THE
BRIDGE PARTY

THE
BRIDGE PARTY

A Play By
SANDRA SEATON

For Sandra,
Great meeting you. Thank
You for your wonderful
work.
Sandra Seaton
2/25/17

EAST END PRESS

THE BRIDGE PARTY

This is a play about the world behind the veil, a glimpse of the black middle class during segregation, when few whites entered the homes of families like the Edwards. The play attempts to recreate the speech and atmosphere of southern black middle-class life in the nineteen-forties. The pace is slow, creating an effect of formality.

Setting: The sitting room of the Edwards home on East End Street in Delphi, a small town in middle Tennessee. The house, built by the parents of Emma Webster Edwards before the Civil War, sits at the top of East Hill on a large plot of land. It is a typical middle-class Southern black home of the time: immaculate, well-maintained, with handed-down furnishings and mementos. The room expresses a sensibility influenced by both Southern gentility and an African sense of design. This African American eclecticism reveals a special flair, an artistic touch that resists definition. Although there is no hint of garishness, the crowded quality of the sitting room suggests that interior decoration has relieved a pent-up need for self-expression when few other avenues were possible.

As the play opens, we see a suite of Victorian furniture--a settee trimmed with delicately carved mahogany and two matching chairs, all of well-worn, faded bottle-green velvet. The high ceilings in the sitting room serve to offset the large scale of the pieces. A low marble table in front of the settee holds a Bible, a Tennessee A&I yearbook, and two small paper fans. On either side of the table, the two matching chairs face each other. To the left of the settee is a tile fireplace--white with tiny green flecks--handmade by the father, Will. Family photographs, ornately framed, an occasional tintype, and a small mirror have been grouped on the wall over the fireplace. On our right, two straight-back oak chairs with padded leather seats stand behind the settee, next to a tall curtained window that looks onto the front porch. Across the room to our left, another window, identical in height, stands next to a bookcase. A doorway to the left of the fireplace leads to a bedroom. Next to the bedroom door is an entrance leading to a long hallway and the kitchen. Off to the right side of the living room stands a player piano stacked high with boxes of piano rolls. A doorway to the right of the piano leads to the front door. A phone without a dial rests on a small wall shelf near the piano. Paul Laurence Dunbar's *Lyrics of Lowly Life* has been tucked away in an opening under the shelf. A walnut victrola sits on a table covered with a fringed commemorative armed forces scarf of deep blue satin; beside the victrola is a stack of records. The usual crocheted doilies are absent, but two large velvet tapestry pillows on a window seat behind and to the left of the settee, are perfectly arranged and unsoiled. Next to the window stands a barrister's bookcase filled with newspapers and books, among them copies of the *Nashville Globe*, college texts, old A&I yearbooks, *American Negro Songs* by J. W. Work, *The Complete Poems of Paul Laurence Dunbar*, James Weldon Johnson's *God's Trombones*, and a pocket Longfellow.

Three tables are set up in the living room for the weekly meeting of the "Saturday Afternoon Bridgettes." Because of the segregation laws enforced in public places, African Americans have developed their own social system, in which clubs like the Bridgettes play an important role. Most of the women in the club are school teachers. One, Pett Mae, is the wife of a prominent black doctor. Ruth, a mortician, has continued the family business after the death of her husband. Leona, Theodora, and four guests, all club members, are playing three-handed bridge.

The Edwards sisters are the hosts; the guests are Pett Mae, Eva Zoe, Samuella, and Ruth. Two tables positioned in the foreground are in use. Theodora, Eva Zoe, and Samuella are seated at the table on our right. Leona, Pett Mae, and Ruth are seated at the table on the left. Players at one table respond, sometimes with quiet laughter, to the conversation at another table. The third table is set off a little from the others and is empty.

Time: 1942--A Saturday afternoon in July. A number of local men are away in the armed services. Will and Emma Edwards' two sons, Morris and Leon, are serving in the Army Air Corps. Randolph Nicholson, Theodora's husband, is at an Army base in California. Leona Barnes's husband, Calvin, is on his way overseas.

CHARACTERS

EMMA EDWARDS, 59, mother of Leona, Marietta, and Theodora

LEONA EDWARDS BARNES, 29

MARIETTA EDWARDS, 27

THEODORA EDWARDS NICHOLSON, 22

MARY JANE BARNES, 58, Leona's mother-in-law

PETT MAE, 39, guest

RUTH, 34, guest

EVA ZOE, 23, guest

SAMUELLA, 39, guest

TOWNSEND, 58, temporary sheriff's deputy

FRANK BYRD, 24, a temporary sheriff's deputy

ACT ONE

[Leona, who appears to be uncomfortable, is arching her back away from the spine of the chair. Her hair is freshly done in croquignole curls, a style popular with black women of her generation. She wears a print crepe dress, muted in color with lace at the bodice, one she would never wear when she is teaching at Macedonia Hill School. A pretty young woman with light brown skin, she is the only one of the sisters who has to straighten her hair. Although she is in the eighth month of pregnancy, she wears her usual clothes, with only the slightest adjustment; few would suspect she is about to have a child. Her only jewelry, a diamond ring on a gold chain, hangs around her neck. From time to time she fingers it nervously. A paper fan of the sort passed out by funeral homes is beside her.]

LEONA: Theodora, where's Marietta and those sandwiches? I told her . . . shrimp salad sandwiches and spiced tea. Shrimp salad and tea.

[Pett Mae, a large woman with very light skin and short, bobbed hair, is the wife of the more prominent of the two local black doctors and a teacher at the black elementary school. Stately rather than blatantly sensual, she could not be described as either an "earth mother" or a "big fine mama." She laughs to herself often and hums constantly as she plays cards. Pett Mae has a high lilting voice; she likes to trill her words. Occasionally, she gestures with a white linen handkerchief. As she listens to Leona, she fumbles with the cards, organizing them in her hand.]

PETT MAE: Be sweet now, Leona. You look real cool and pretty. Real sweet. Anybody'd think you carried on this way all the time.

[Ruth, who is seated on the right side of Leona, places her hand firmly under Leona's arm. A mortician who has continued the family business after the death of her husband, Ruth still retains all the vitality and freshness of a new bride. She can be playful one moment, serious and plainspoken the next. Ruth is tall and sturdily built, with deep brown skin, even and rich in color, and startlingly white teeth. Since an illness in her early twenties, she sits with one leg pulled up and walks with a limp, which at times becomes a dance. She is dressed in a white tea length gown with long full sleeves, single-pleated from shoulder to the wrist on both sides; the skirt drapes to allow her to sit gracefully.]

RUTH: Now Pett, she can't help it.

PETT MAE: Just be sweet, real sweet.

[Eva Zoe, who is seated with Theodora and Samuella at the opposite table, calls out to Leona. Eva Zoe, also a teacher, was Theodora's college roommate at Tennessee A & I. She wears a dress of vermillion red, small pearl earrings, and thin gold bracelets that slide back and forth when she moves. A raffia purse, tightly woven with strips of bright cotton, is beside her at the table. Unlike the other women, Eva Zoe wears rouge, but not so much as to appear excessive. A three-cornered, veiled Mr. John hat is perched at an angle to one side of her full bangs.]

EVA ZOE: Listen to Pett, Leona.

RUTH: Right now she just can't.

LEONA: You know those little tea sandwiches . . . you take a sharp knife right across the edge, takes the crust right off. You hold them like little diamonds, then you cut them down the middle into teeniny diamonds. **[She gently**

twines the gold chain at her neck.]

[Theodora, after trying without success to concentrate on the bridge game, examines her cards again, then, like a teacher starting the first morning class, raps them against her open hand. Tall, statuesque, light-skinned, with long slender limbs, she has the looks of a movie star of the forties. All the sisters are considered attractive, but Theodora is thought to be the most beautiful.]

THEODORA: Two tables of three handed bridge. When's the rest of the bunch gonna get here?

LEONA: You hold them like little diamonds, then you cut them down the middle. **[She continues to finger the gold chain at her neck.]**

THEODORA: Leona, Marietta's been making shrimp salad sandwiches for years. Somebody, hurry up. Bid so I can get up and help serve.

RUTH: Whoa now, Theodora. You're just like one of those thoroughbred race horses. I swear you Edwards all race around. Cleanest house I've ever seen. You all must sweep and clean all day.

PETT MAE: Oh my! Will you look at this hand?

LEONA: Theodora's been up since five this morning sweeping and washing.

RUTH: That Theodora. She's a fast one.

THEODORA: Getting ready for my trip. **[Feels forehead, as if trying to hold back some mounting pain.]**

LEONA: Theodora gets up sweepin'. I used to sweep all the

time myself . . . couldn't stand to see anything on the floor.

PETT MAE: Slam! We don't need to play this one out, ladies. All that carryin' on. **[Pett Mae laughs to herself.** Spades--ace, king, queen . . .

[Theodora, disgusted, picks up cards and shuffles the deck.]

LEONA: If Marietta doesn't hurry up, I'll start sweeping myself.

EVA ZOE: That's a pretty dress, Leona.

LEONA: I used to sweep all the time . . . just don't feel like it lately.

EVA ZOE: Your dress, Leona, it sure is nice.

LEONA: Willie C. gave it to me. Said they wouldn't let her wear it to teach. Said they wouldn't let me teach in it either. She told me to keep it, wear it to club meeting. Before Willie C. went out West, remember, Eva Zoe, how she used to sit at that piano over there, beaux crowded all around? Willie C. always did have beautiful clothes.

EVA ZOE: Well, it sure looks pretty on you.

LEONA: Pretty or not, Professor Sampson Barnes don't 'low no dresses with lace at his school.

RUTH: Yes, Professor Barnes.

PETT MAE: Well, we're bidding this afternoon, ladies, not teaching. Better leave the professor out of the game.

[The women laugh.]

LEONA: Leave him out? If he saw me teaching in this, lace all around the neck—as soon as school was out, he'd march right home and tell it: "Mary Jane, oh, Mary Jane. Calvin's wife was over there showin' out." It's a good thing my mother-in-law can't see me. She'd be carryin' on right now.

PETT MAE: Little bird . . .

LEONA: I tell you, it's a good thing.

PETT MAE: Little bird, you married Sampson and Mary Jane's son . . .

LEONA: Married.

PETT MAE: That's right, married. You married Mary Jane's son, not the whole family.

LEONA: Calvin? Getting ready to go overseas with the rest of the boys. Carrying a big stack of letters, everyone of 'em from his mother. She's been telling him all sorts of things. **[Trails off into her own thoughts.]**

THEODORA: Pett . . . **[Fumbles with her cards.]** shoot, pass me that box of talcum powder.

RUTH: **[to Theodora]** You're as jittery as a little bug. **[Begins to hum "Pony Boy" up and under.]**

LEONA: Randy, handsome as he is, away from home.

[Ruth continues to hum.]

THEODORA: I'm gonna sprinkle these cards. Get 'em to shuffle a little.

PETT MAE: I bet Randy boy's late with his letter.

[Samuella, a teacher and an Oberlin graduate, is an elegant woman who seems a little more formal than the rest. She wears glasses on a chain and has a thin silver streak in her hair. Her mauve gown, with its short fitted sleeves and set of three diagonal pleats across the bodice, flatters her coloring.]

SAMUELLA: A young husband all the way out in California.

LEONA: Theodora sweeps and sweeps.

RUTH: **[Begins to sing "Pony Boy." Continues to sing while the women are talking.]** Pony boy, pony boy won't you be my pony boy, giddiup, giddiup, giddiup, whoa, my pony boy. She's a thoroughbred alright.

LEONA: You can tell when Theodora's worried.

PETT MAE: She tries to look real cool, but we all know better.

LEONA: You can tell by how hard she sweeps.

RUTH: Don't tell Theodora that.

[Theodora sticks out her tongue at Pett Mae. Music fades out.]

PETT MAE: I'm an old bird, can't fool me. Give Theodora--Miss Thoroughbred--the powder.

THEODORA: *Mrs.* Thoroughbred.

SAMUELLA: Correction noted.

[Her glasses slip and dangle on their chain.]

PETT MAE: [to Theodora] Mrs. Thoroughbred. Doctor's first wife used to put powder on a handkerchief.

["A Tisket A Tasket" up and under.]

RUTH: What'd she do that for?

PETT MAE: She'd put it on the handkerchief and slide it down her girdle.

THEODORA: Her girdle?

PETT MAE: That's right, Theodora.

THEODORA: I'd never wear one of those.

PETT MAE: She sure did . . . in her girdle, so she wouldn't stick to herself when she played whist.

[Theodora laughs.]

RUTH: The heat'll do that. [Pulls at her dress, adjusts herself in her seat.]

[All the women laugh except Leona, who twists uncomfortably. Music fades out. Car sounds can be heard.]

SAMUELLA: Leona, where's that letter everyone's been going on about?

THEODORA: It wasn't a letter, Sam. Calvin Barnes sent us that blue pillow cover over there.

EVA ZOE: It was really for Leona.

SAMUELLA: [Points to the pillow cover on the table.]

The satin one, the one with the Army Air Corp insignia?

EVA ZOE: [**Goes over and touches cloth.**] Look at that fringe. He's trying to get back in Leona's good graces.

LEONA: Seems like half the town, everybody we know's going to war. I hear they're real hard on the colored boys. Throw them in jail. Send them to some kind of camp. Just like that! Theodora, when you go out there with Randy, you think you'll see Calvin?

THEODORA: Calvin Barnes? He's on his way overseas. I've got the worst headache.

SAMUELLA: Lord knows, Leona, if you don't stop all this carrying on . . . Pett, how did Doctor put it . . . about nerves in the summertime?

EVA ZOE: Miss Samuella, so proper, you know it's more than that.

PETT MAE: Cool down now, ladies. Remember, you don't have to bid if you don't have anything.

LEONA: Marietta! Oh, Marietta . . .

[**Country western music plays in the background. Eva Zoe hums along.**]

LEONA: She's out there listening to the Opry. Marietta!

EVA ZOE: [**Continues to hum.**] Singin' along with Mr. Deford Bailey.

THEODORA: Eva Zoe--bid!

EVA ZOE: It's Opry time!

THEODORA: The Opry in broad daylight??!! Now will you bid?

PETT MAE: Ladies, ladies. Tend to your hands. Too early for the Opry.

LEONA: Well, I wish Marietta would come on. You know I have to keep her straight. The last time she made those little sandwiches she used tongue.

PETT MAE: Oh ho.

SAMUELLA: Used to be that's all people fixed.

LEONA: Chopped it so fine you couldn't tell.

THEODORA: You didn't know the difference, Leona.

LEONA: That's not the point.

RUTH: Marietta can fix anything. Bet she coulda used my old shoe.

THEODORA: And Leona can eat anything.

LEONA: Should've been shamed of herself, said "Oh you're gonna love this, Leona. It'll melt in your mouth."

RUTH: I bet it tasted like your Papa's catfish.

LEONA: Well, if that's the kind of fish he catches, Papa can keep it.

THEODORA: Leona, shh! Papa's gone to Nashville, taking President Hale and the doctors from Meharry fishing, just to help put food on the table.

LEONA: Well, he can. Ate that stuff Marietta fixed like a

little baby eating pablum . . . every bit. Then she tips in and says "Oh, by the way, Leona, it's tongue." I could have died.

[Theodora and Ruth laugh.]

Papa spoils us, brings us whatever we want. No man will ever be like him.

THEODORA: I'll miss him when I leave.

LEONA: Don't say that, Theodora. Not now.

RUTH: You all are grown. Not many can outdo the Edwards . . . Theodora and Leona teaching. Marietta and Emma working too.

PETT MAE: All living under the same roof. That's a fortune.

EVA ZOE: No wonder Leona bought that beaver coat last Christmas.

LEONA: Eva Zoe, you bought one too. All the gang did, just like follow the leader. Theodora, you looked like a starlet in yours.

EVA ZOE: Like one of those Dandridge sisters. What's her name?

RUTH: Just like I said, Leona, we're grown women, taking care of ourselves.

LEONA: I'm on my own. **[Stops suddenly. Startled expression, as if she is thinking of the idea for the first time.]**

[Women all stop talking.]

PETT MAE: You'll get by, little bird.

LEONA: Not when it's like this--it's hard. Poor Agnes, she's by herself too, ever since Frank passed. I guess that's why she's not here.

PETT MAE: Doctor did all he could.

RUTH: Don't tell a soul--I paid for Frank's suit myself.

PETT MAE: Ruth had it hard.

RUTH: Now, Pett . . .

PETT MAE: Doesn't have Jim around to help with the bodies.

RUTH: When the call comes, I go out, middle of the night, doesn't matter. I go right over to the family. This leg of mine aches so, sometimes I take a cane. Last Friday, I went from home to home. They're always waiting, with a cup of coffee, to sit, talk things over.

LEONA: You have to work hard on the bodies, don't you Ruth? You and Jim . . .

PETT MAE: Jim's gone, Leona.

LEONA: **[Turns to Ruth.]** Now your husband's gone. All our boys. They're gone too. Randy in the army out in California. Calvin on his way overseas. You have to do all the business yourself, Ruth. Take care of all of it, call on the families.

THEODORA: Ruth always did dress the bodies.

PETT MAE: And washed and pressed the hair. She styles it the same way they always wore it, even picks their favorite color, makeup and all.

SAMUELLA: I can still picture my mother's gown.

LEONA: You all, you all, remember last New Year's Day, how it snowed and snowed and snowed and all you all came by in Doctor's brand-new Buick? Poor Pett, got stuck in that little bitty curve out front, had to turn around, couldn't even come in the house. Well, that very morning, an undertaker came all the way from Spring Hill, right here to East End Street, just to court Theodora.

SAMUELLA: Spring Hill? Callie Morton's grandson--Mrs. A. J. Morton and Sons Funeral Home? Theodora never told me that.

PETT MAE: An undertaker's high up--can't go much higher.

EVA ZOE: Except for doctors and preachers. If my child married one . . .

RUTH: [to Leona.] We didn't have much time together, not like some folks. After I married Jim his mother took me aside . . . like so. "Girl"--she always called me "Ruth girl"--"close your eyes and picture it . . . Jim , white gloves, fine linen suit, a gold watch chain spilling out. You'll belong to the town. Like one of the family. When the call comes, you'll go to the sick bed, hold a hand. At the church you'll lead the way. The Lord's own shepherd, standing by the aisle, ushering the kinfolk to their seats. The smell of fresh gardenias, so many you can't count them all. Back from the cemetery you'll be served with the family, chicken, baked ham. Press your hair on Saturday morning, tie it up and sweat all day over a hot stove--never! Not as long as you live."

LEONA: You didn't have much time together.

RUTH: Not like some.

LEONA: Jim's gone. V. K., Mary's husband, he's gone too. Two funeral parlors in town and both run by women--and me and Calvin . . . **[Throws down her hand.]**

married a year and already separated. Anything could happen to him all the way over there. Couldn't it? Couldn't it, Ruth?

[Samuella shakes her head, as if embarrassed by Leona's directness. Leona jumps up and speaks to the women directly.]

LEONA: I heard Cordie Cheek's coming back today. **[They don't respond.]** You'all. School'll be starting before you know it. **(No response.)** You hear any news about Cordie Cheek? **(No response)** Where's Marietta? She knows everybody's business but her own.

PETT MAE: These cards are playing real nice, Leona. You better pick up your hand so we can whip these . . . **[She touches her mouth coquettishly with a lace handkerchief.]** "n's" . . . **[Mumbles something and leans back tittering.]**

RUTH: She'll be all right. She tires out these days.

PETT MAE: Just stay real cool and pretty. In the pink. **[Winks.]**

[The women laugh, even Leona.]

RUTH: That gold necklace sure looks lovely with your dress, Leona.

Marietta enters from the kitchen carrying a tray of beverages. Soft-spoken and gentle, she wears a plain, crisply starched shirtwaist dress of faded spring colors, flat sandals with stockings, and a full white apron with pockets across the front. The darkest of all the four sisters, she has deep brown skin, fine features, straight black hair from her mother's Indian heritage, and dimples--not as deep as Theodora's.

[Leona pulls the necklace out of her dress and holds the small diamond ring attached to its chain in the palm of her hand. Meanwhile, Ruth and Pett Mae examine the ring as Marietta approaches the table.

LEONA: Lovely.

RUTH: And that's not all . . . land sakes, look at that ring.

PETT MAE: That's a big one, all right.

RUTH: I'll say.

LEONA: It shines just like a star, an evening star, even in the daytime.

PETT MAE: If push comes to shove, you can pawn it.

[Marietta carries a tray with sandwiches and a pitcher of spiced tea. Leona fidgets in her seat. The other women set their hands aside and wait patiently. An aroma of oranges and cinnamon fills the air. Leona is more anxious than ever to talk to her.]

SAMUELLA: Oranges and cinnamon!

PETT MAE: Here she is, just as sweet as she can be. Our own Sunday School superintendent.

RUTH: Miss Saint Paul A.M.E.

EVA ZOE: When you gonna learn how to play bridge, Marietta?

MARIETTA: I learned all I'm gonna learn, thank you.

THEODORA: Bridge doesn't agree with Marietta's religion.

LEONA: Takes after Grandma. When Grandma was alive, we used to have to lock ourselves in our room just to play cards.

THEODORA: We cut our teeth on cards.

LEONA: Remember the first time Willie C. came home from A & I? We used to hide in her room so she could teach us bridge.

PETT MAE: Marietta thinks church-going folks shouldn't play cards.

MARIETTA: I said no such thing. Suit yourself. Do what you want. Makes me no never mind.

EVA ZOE: There's not a woman in this room that plays cards on Sunday.

[All the women nod.]

LEONA: Marietta, I need to see you for just a minute. Don't take all day. Please. I'm about to burn up.

PETT MAE: [Reaches over and pats Leona on the shoulder.] Sometimes me and Leona, Doctor and Doctor's new helper, Tommy, play cards till midnight on Saturday, then we lay our hands down.

SAMUELLA: Many a slam was ruined by the strike of the clock.

RUTH: Marietta just has those ways. She promised the Lord she wouldn't play cards.

[Marietta brings the tray to Leona.]

LEONA: Finger sandwiches! Marietta--little olives on the side, Oriental pickles and chicken bouillon.

PETT MAE: Now, Leona, be sure and save a little room for Miss Estelle's cake.

LEONA: It's so hot. Just stir the tea and pour it on the ice. That's all I need. Please hurry, Marietta. **[Leona fans herself.]**

MARIETTA: As many folks as I've cooked for, I guess I know how to make iced tea.

[A car can be heard passing by.]

LEONA: All that noise.

[Cars go by again.]

THEODORA: That has to be the boys on their way back from Nashville.

LEONA: Marietta, **[long pause]** Marietta?

MARIETTA: Lord ha'mercy. You 'bout to worry me to death.

LEONA: I heard Cordie Cheek was coming back today. If

he is . . . I heard his trial was over.

MARIETTA: Didn't have a trial. Grand jury up at Nash-ville--all white, every last one of them--they let Cordie Cheek go.

LEONA: Thank the Lord!

PETT MAE: A colored child.

RUTH: Saved.

SAMUELLA: Case dismissed for lack of evidence. **[Removes glasses.]** Deliberated and refused to indict.

MARIETTA: They'll be whoopin' and hollerin' when Cordie Cheek gets to town. Mr. Saul Blanton'll be doin' plenty of business. Sellin' plenty of liquor tonight.

PETT MAE: Not just to his own bunch, either.

MARIETTA: When the law comes back, they'll want what he's sellin'. Come morning, Mr. Saul Blanton'll know all *their* business.

[Cars go by.]

RUTH: Every Jim and Mandy, they'll be headin' up to ol' King Saul's, fiddlin' till the sun comes up.

EVA ZOE: Colored and white.

MARIETTA: White folks go to a colored bootlegger, they leave their money and a whole lot more. A bootlegger, he stays real quiet. Sits up all hours of the night. Hardly rests at all. Anytime folks need a loan, have to get outa town, you better find him. He'll make the folks up to the court-house understand what you need, the only way they know to, with the dollar. You in trouble, you best to ask Mr. Saul.

LEONA: Marietta, what about the Lord?

[Samuella leans forward in her seat.]

MARIETTA: The Lord helps those who help themselves.

LEONA: Marietta . . .

MARIETTA: Oh, hush and drink your tea.

LEONA: I can't.

MARIETTA: Oh, go on, gal.

LEONA: I can't. I can't just sit here. I won't be still till that boy Cordie Cheek comes back to town.

THEODORA: I bet it's the Alphas. Randy's an Alpha.

MARIETTA: Didn't say a thing about no Alphas.

[More cars go by.]

RUTH: I didn't know the Alphas made all that commotion.

PETT MAE: Ask the fraternity sweetheart.

EVA ZOE: Little Miss Ivy.

THEODORA: It's after the game. You know how every-body gets . . . after the game.

LEONA: If Cordie Cheek comes back today, all the folks'll be out to see him--all of Macedonia School.

RUTH: His ma . . .

LEONA: Miss Tenny.

RUTH: She'll jump for joy.

[The screen door starts to open slightly. The women look up. Marietta sets the empty tray next to Leona and walks past the piano to the front door to investigate.]

THEODORA: Maybe that's the rest of the bunch. The game's over by now. If Punk and Mrs. Hawthorne get back from Nashville in time, we can still get the prize for attendance.

[Mary Jane Barnes, Leona's mother-in-law, enters. Consciously old-fashioned, she wears a plain dress, drab purple in color, with a high collar and tiny buttons up to her neck--a style she considers appropriate for the wife of the principal of Macedonia Hill School. She does not conceal her hostility to the group.

MARIETTA: Make yourself comfortable, Miss Mary Jane. Rest a spell. How you and Professor Barnes gettin' along?

[Mary Jane was angry when she arrived, but now her anger is increased by the sight of the women playing cards. She glares disapprovingly at Leona, Leona begins to fan herself more rapidly. The women at the tables look at Mary Jane, then Leona.]

Every Saturday afternoon, you know, the "Bridgettes," they meet at a different house, every Saturday. **[Marietta points to the empty table.]** Didn't get the crowd we usually do. You know Pett Mae, your doctor's wife, and Ruth, Jim passed away. She's the mortician now herself. They're sittin' at the front table.

MARY JANE: Hush up! Been knowin' that one since I

taught her in first grade. **[Points to Eva Zoe.]** And that one and that one over there. Every last one of you.

EVA ZOE: **[Stands up.]** Miss Mary Jane, I just love your dress. **[Sits down slowly.]** Never will be a teacher like Miss Mary Jane.

[Leona arches her back and pulls away from the chair. She clutches her necklace tightly. The women arrange their hands. Mary Jane stands for a minute, then moves toward the straight-backed oak chair off to the corner.]

MARIETTA: Mama'll be home t'rectly, Miss Mary Jane.

[Mary Jane sits down in the chair. Leona stares intently at Theodora until Theodora becomes uncomfortable. Theodora gets up, goes to a victrola and picks a record from a stack. She plays "Take the A-Train" by the Duke Ellington Orchestra.]

SAMUELLA: Theodora would come up with that one. The theme for the club dance.

EVA ZOE: Remember our last formal?

SAMUELLA: Presenting the "Bridgettes" of Delphi, Tennessee . . .

EVA ZOE: We were dressed to kill.

[The women applaud and laugh. Mary Jane watches them closely, then picks up a book and raps it on the side of her chair.]

MARY JANE: Eva Zoe, wipe that red mess off your face. You can see it all the way through the window.

[Eva Zoe reaches for her purse, pulls out a compact and checks her makeup.]

PETT MAE: Better have something cool, Mary Jane. Doctor wouldn't want you all hot and . . .

[The women cast furtive glances at Mary Jane and then look away.]

PETT MAE: Theodora always did pick the latest.

RUTH: She's a thoroughbred all right. **[Hums and snaps her fingers at Theodora.]** "Take the A-Train" . . . that's Ellington's song.

EVA ZOE: Leona can sing it for our summer dance . . . for the Bridgettes.

SAMUELLA: Takes after Mother Emma, the finest songstress in middle Tennessee.

RUTH: Go on over to the piano, Pett. Leona, you sing.

PETT MAE: That's a hard one . . . how does that go? **[Pett Mae hums to herself, but remains in her seat, arranging her bridge hand.]**

RUTH: Oh, Leona can sing anything.

EVA ZOE: And eat anything too.

[All the women laugh except for Leona and Mary Jane.]

PETT MAE: Remember when Leona sang at the club dance?

EVA ZOE: Calvin Barnes was in the front row.

PETT MAE: She was wearing that blue crepe dress, the one with the gold hobnails across the front . . . so cool looking.

EVA ZOE: Like a dream.

RUTH: Hello, Nashville.

SAMUELLA: Our regional meeting.

RUTH: President Pett Mae Crosley-Gaines, pullin' up in Doctor's big Buick.

[Fadeout "A-Train." "A Tisket, A Tasket" up and under.]

SAMUELLA: The majordomo of the clan.

RUTH: All of you, the whole gang piled in. Leona, me and Miss--Mrs. Jitterbug up front, Eva Zoe, Sam, Punk.

EVA ZOE: We were doin' some scootin', weren't we, Pett?

PETT MAE: Old Harry Gordon, Doctor's best patient, went all the way to New York for those dresses. I woke him up bright and early that Saturday morning.

THEODORA: Before the rooster crowed.

PETT MAE: **[Pretends to hold phone to ear.]** "Rise on up. Open that store so we can pick up that girl's dress on the way to Nashville."

RUTH: When she walked in on Calvin Barnes's arm, didn't she turn a head or two?

EVA ZOE: It sure did fit her nice.

LEONA: Nice is right. I bet you I couldn't teach in it.

[Music stops. Mary Jane turns sharply and looks at Leona, then turns away, wringing her hands nervously.]

MARIETTA: Rheumatism flaring up, Miss Mary Jane?

[Marietta leaves room and enters again with glasses of iced tea. Theodora rises and helps serve the tea. The other women murmur approval as they drink.]

PETT MAE: Doctor's orders, Mary Jane. **[She motions to Theodora to give a glass to Mary Jane.]**

LEONA: This tea sure does cool me off. Keeps my hair from going back. Always did wish I had your hair, Theodora.

[Theodora smiles. Leona mouths words silently and fumbles with her necklace. The necklace with its ring comes loose and falls to the floor. Mary Jane stands up and tries to see what's going on. Marietta serves tea to the second table, then sets a tray with four glasses at the empty table.]

MARIETTA: Mama always said you were marked. **[Walks to the front, picks up the necklace. She speaks loudly, as if to distract attention from her actions.]**

THEODORA: Who was marked?

MARIETTA: Leona. Leona was.

THEODORA: Oh, Marietta.

MARIETTA: She was. Mama said when she was carrying Leona, she used to go across the street over where Miss

Cora used to live. Went there all the time. Said Miss Cora's little girl was real dark, had real nappy hair. Mama said the little girl marked her.

LEONA: Marietta, you oughta be shot.

EVA ZOE: Miss Mary Jane fixes hair right out of her house. She's heard of it too, haven't you, Miss Mary Jane?

[Mary Jane strains to hear every word.]

MARY JANE: Eva Zoe Walker, look at you--face greased, like somebody threw a bucket of paint all over you!

PETT MAE: Stay cool now, Mary Jane.

MARY JANE: Hair all curled up, fried . . . it's bad for the nerves. Women come to me, they get nothing but a warm comb.

[Eva Zoe hides her face with cards. Marietta walks over to Leona to hand her the ring. Mary Jane gets up and follows Marietta. When Marietta turns around abruptly, Mary Jane goes back to her seat. Mary Jane watches Marietta but isn't able to see what she is handing Leona.]

MARIETTA: Leona, when you were born, Mama said you had the nappiest hair she'd ever seen.

[Women at both tables giggle to themselves.]

LEONA: Everybody's heard that.

RUTH: Oh hush, Marietta.

THEODORA: Marietta always did tell stories.

RUTH: No tellin' what she'll come up with.

MARIETTA: I mind my own business, thank you.

THEODORA: Marietta always did tell things.

MARIETTA: *Did*, Miss Ivy.

LEONA: Like that one about Papa stealin' a pig and hidin' it up on Professor Barnes's roof…

MARIETTA: I wadn't but twelve.

LEONA: Don't matter. You told it.

MARIETTA: Nappy or not, the professor used to chase all us home.

LEONA: Mother always did have beautiful hair. Papa has that fine soft hair. Mother never could figure out how I got this hair. **[sincerely]** Calvin used to tease me, tease me all the time about my hair. Didn't he, Miss Mary Jane?

MARIETTA: They say when you're carryin' a child and certain folks get too near you, they mark you--for life. Said when she was carrying you, used to go over to Miss Cora's all the time. They say you have to be careful when you're carrying a child. Don't they, Pett?

[When Mary Jane stands up abruptly, her glass slips from her hand and shatters on the floor. She starts to pick up the pieces, then straightens up and marches out of the room. The front door can be heard slamming. Theodora rushes to sweep up the broken glass. Eva Zoe goes over to Leona, alternately whispering and laughing nervously. The women calmly begin to play cards again. Marietta busies herself removing the dishes and

straightening the room.]

PETT MAE: That bird was movin'.

MARIETTA: Miss Mary Jane's one of those old-timey folks.

EVA ZOE: That's right, don't mess with Miss Mary Jane.

PETT MAE: Never saw one fly off the handle like that.

SAMUELLA: I don't think Miss Mary Jane approves of you ladies.

EVA ZOE: Speak for yourself, Sam.

PETT MAE: That bird wanted something from one of Emma Edwards' high yellow daughters.

MARIETTA: "Wanted" is right. Miss Mary Jane woulda been singin' all the way to Happy Hollow if that ring Leona dropped on the floor was in her pocketbook right now.

SAMUELLA: **[to Theodora]** Mother Emma better not hear about you all running Miss Mary Jane out.

THEODORA: I'm bidding two hearts.

LEONA: Three diamonds. **[Turns to Ruth.]**

RUTH: Pass.

[Eva Zoe is looking into space, as if still thinking about Mary Jane's visit. Theodora glances at her sideways.]

PETT MAE: Look at these cards! Come on, ladies! The honeymoon's over.

RUTH: Used to be Miss Mary Jane didn't worry so much about other folks.

THEODORA: Eva Zoe! [Theodora nudges Eva Zoe.]

EVA ZOE: Hasn't been the same since she stopped teaching, started doing hair out of her house. She . . .

MARIETTA: Hasn't been the same since Uncle Sam caught up with her boy.

THEODORA: Well, she didn't get what she came for. Eva Zoe--I said two hearts.

[Eva Zoe laughs out loud, snaps to attention, and throws hands in air dramatically, as if to surrender.]

RUTH: [to Theodora] All right, Miss Jitterbug. Leona--Leona, what you gonna do?

LEONA: I already bid.

RUTH: I don't mean that.

MARIETTA: Go on back with him. Might as well. He makes a good living.

THEODORA: [excited] Why can't Leona leave town? --- go off somewhere else.

RUTH: He's a teacher, Theodora. She'd have whatever she wanted right here in Delphi!

PETT MAE: A fine home.

MARIETTA: Might as well stay. Some things just meant to be.

THEODORA: But Marietta, what if they can't get along?

PETT MAE: Married to a big-shot Kappa. Look at that ring. Anything I got while I was married, I'd keep.

LEONA: I never said a thing about giving anything up. **[clutching necklace]**

THEODORA: Sometimes women just have to leave anyway.

MARIETTA: When I ran off with Joe Harlan, I didn't have a thing in my suitcase but Grandma's old hymnal book . . . and that satin nightgown from Sears, Roebuck, four sizes too big. Grandma couldn't stand Joe, so we ran off.

RUTH: The superintendent of the Sunday School.

LEONA: I still can't imagine Marietta running off with anybody.

SAMUELLA: Running off. I wouldn't say that . . . no, I wouldn't say that. Eloping, that's better.

MARIETTA: Papa told me to go to college, to A & I. I had to go off and get married. Didn't last either. I've been working as a cook and a nurse ever since.

LEONA: You never look back, Marietta.

MARIETTA: Well, it's done. No use talking 'bout it now. Shoulda thought about it then. You make your bed hard, you lie in it. Too late now.

LEONA: Not for my mother-in-law. If she comes back here, I swear I'll . . . She sure does wear me out.

THEODORA: She can't bother you as long as we're here.

SAMUELLA: Mother Emma won't let her.

LEONA: Doctor's gonna want to see me before the end of the week. The way I'm feeling, it might be time.

PETT MAE: You little birds have to be careful. Doctor wouldn't have it any other way. **[Sprinkles more powder on the cards.]**

RUTH: Right after Eugene was born they had a dance over to the Elks. Doctor told me not to go. Went out wearing a real thin chiffon dress, caught the flu. They had to put me to bed for a month. When I got out the bed, this leg here, it didn't have a bit of feeling. Just started to draw up. I been limping ever since.

PETT MAE: **[to Leona]** Always say to B. F., "Doctor, what must that one do?" He'll always say "Care, just a little care."

THEODORA: Hear that, Leona? You have to be careful. Can't go having a taste for everything, then acting fretful just because you can't have it. Look at you whinin' and carryin' on . . . by the time the rest of the gang gets here . . . you won't be worth a dime.

[Theodora gets up and starts to tidy room. Marietta adjusts chairs at empty table, walks to the front and leaves. Theodora walks to spotlight. Fadeout on other lights.]

THEODORA: All this old furniture . . . Every time we have club meeting, there's hardly room to put up the card tables. Grandma's folks--out at the Thatcher Plantation--when she first got married, they sent all this out here. You know how velvet gets when it's old and faded. Just like the inside of a casket. Willie C.--that's my oldest sister--she used to teach over at Macedonia Hill. When she got her first paycheck, she went right out and put the money down on that player piano over in the corner. She always did know how to have a high time. Said she was tired of all this small town stuff. Everybody out in California has that new Spanish style, at least that's what Willie C. says.

About Leona--both our brothers, they're gone, over-seas. Calvin Barnes, he's on his way over there too. That's part of it . . . they put the thing about Cordie Cheek in the *Nashville Globe*. Leona keeps the whole paper, the one about that boy, right by her bed. She's taking it real hard. If Papa was here, she'd settle down. Papa . . . when he takes the white sportsmen out on his boat, they toe the line. "Mr. Edwards," that's what they call him--and he'll leave you if you're a minute late. 1939--the year I went to A & I--Papa sent me his yellow raincoat.

[Theodora's music, "Take the A-Train," begins.] All the bands that came to Nashville signed it. Erskine Hawkins and the 'Bama State Collegians, Jimmie Lunce-ford, Count Basie. I had those big city boys signing all over the back of that coat. I'd turn around like this. They'd write their names right here. **[Points to back of coat.]** Me, Willie C., Leona, Eva Zoe--half the town went to A & I, our half the town, that is. I was the fraternity sweetheart, too. All the Alphas said it was because I had the deepest dimples and the straightest teeth they'd ever seen. They're always saying I look like somebody. Now it's one of the Dandridge sisters. Dorothy . . . that's it, Dorothy Dandridge. **[Touches forehead. She's having a headache.]** I've never been late for anything in my life. And I don't plan to be late leaving.

[Spotlight fades, music fades. Bring up lights on bridge players. The women in the room continue their bridge game. Emma enters from the front door, clutching a white apron tightly in one hand.

*Emma is the mother of four daughters, Leona, Marietta,
Theodora and Willie C., and two sons, Leon and Morris.
Like many African American women of her generation, she
is a mixture of African, Indian and white. A slender, elegant woman with medium-brown skin and heavy black
straight hair, Emma wears a breezy looking summer dress,
the skirt just full enough to move easily as she walks. With
a cameo brooch at the neck and her hair pulled back into a
chignon, she could be coming from an afternoon tea. She
speaks and gestures with a dramatic flair that becomes a
weapon in difficult situations.]*

EMMA: Howdy, y'all.

WOMEN: Howdy, Mama Emma.

**[They murmur respectfully in unison. The conversation
has the quality of call and response used in the black
church.]**

EMMA: Mary Jane's after me. I was walking up the hill,
when lo and behold if Mary Jane didn't come walking right
up behind me. **[Mischievous expression, as if starting to
tell a wicked story.]** I was walking along, kicking up the
dust . . .

[Mary Jane enters suddenly.]

MARY JANE: Just the one I was lookin' for.

EMMA: **[Turns, looks at audience.]** What did I tell you?
She was right behind me.

MARY JANE: I was right behind her.

EMMA: Sure was hot out there.

RUTH: Up to the white Methodist church, Mamma Emma?

EMMA: There too.

MARY JANE: I followed her every step.

EMMA: So I turned and whipped around the corner. I said to myself, I'm goin' to see how my Leona's doing.

MARY JANE: That's where I was going too.

EMMA: It was mighty hot . . . down at that kitchen.

MARY JANE: **[negatively]** The Methodist church.

EMMA: You girls know Viola McCoy?

RUTH: The judge's wife?

EMMA: Well, Viola McCoy up and starts with me: "Now Emma, this here is a book on how to set the table. I 'spects you would enjoy it."

LEONA: Everybody knows about women like Mrs. McCoy.

EMMA: She told me just the other day--you know I just listened, didn't say a word--"Now Emma, if you just come down and cook us our meal, you won't have to wash nary a dish." **[Stops short. Hands on hips, theatrically.]** Biggest liar I've ever seen.

THEODORA: Now, mother.

LEONA: Calling Mrs. McCoy a liar . . . Mother.

THEODORA: Mother sure does like to perform.

LEONA: Mother always has wanted to be on the stage.

RUTH: Have some iced tea, Mama Emma.

EMMA: That's all right, darlin'. **[Pats Ruth on hand.]**
Your mama'll be all right. Have some iced tea, Mary Jane.

MARY JANE: Emma, there's a thing or two . . .

EMMA: Mind your glass, Mary Jane. **[Emma begins to
sip tea.]** Will's gone fishing with the doctors from Meharry.
I got Leona. Don't know what I can do for you.

**[The sound of cars going by can be heard. The women
all look towards the window.]**

LEONA: Sure is a lot of commotion around here. When it's
hot, in the summer when the screens are in, you can hear
everything in the world.

MARY JANE: Everything.

LEONA: It was spring the last time I saw Cordie Cheek.

THEODORA: It's those boys from out of town racin' up
and down the hill again.

MARIETTA: Thought it was the Alphas.

THEODORA: The Alphas? All that noise? It's that old
bunch from out of town.

PETT MAE: Every time Tuskegee plays A & I they run
through here. Bad as poor . . .

LEONA: That's where everybody goes, over to Tuskegee to
get married.

MARY JANE: That's where you went with my son.

LEONA: **[off in her own world]** The day before Easter.

MARY JANE: It was wet and cold.

LEONA: When we went to Tuskegee, I had to wrap a coat around myself. I wore my silk crepe dress. The one Aunt Ellen sent from Detroit, a peach color, soft, draped.

THEODORA: Sure did. You got all those clothes. The same size as that lady Aunt Ellen works for.

MARY JANE: It's been six months since you talked to my boy.

LEONA: Calvin . . .

MARY JANE: I've got a thing or two to say . . .

LEONA: In front of all these people.

MARY JANE: In a small town, everybody finds out anyway.

LEONA: All right, it's been six months since he went home to your house. I moved my things out first. We didn't live at Miss Estelle's a year.

SAMUELLA: Mother Emma, don't let her come in here . . .

EMMA: **[Addresses women in an exaggerated way, as though she is performing a role.]** Girl hardly grown trying to sass our guest. Now Mary Jane darlin', don't carry on so.

MARY JANE: What did you expect? Her not knowing how

to take care of a house. Calvin was used to having everything kept up.

LEONA: I was good to your boy.

MARY JANE: Girl . . . did you or did you not bring him
down here every day?

LEONA: This is my house, too, Miss Mary Jane.

MARY JANE: To your mother's house to eat his dinner?

LEONA: I was a grown woman teaching out at Morning
Star, out in the country. By the time I got home . . .

EMMA: My daughter's not on trial.

MARY JANE: To your mother's house to eat his evening
meal.

LEONA: Mother always had the supper ready.

MARY JANE: A wife's place is at home. Not out in the
country somewhere. Is this the way you brought her up? Is
this how you raised this girl?

SAMUELLA: Mother Emma . . .

EMMA: Be still, girl. Give a visiting mother-in-law her
due.

MARY JANE: A wife's place . . .

LEONA: A wife's place? He never complained about that. I
taught out at Theta, Morning Star . . . when we lived at
Miss Estelle's, I paid my part--four rooms, half the house.
Was that my place? Things were fine when I was out in the
country. The little school children, they hung on my every

word. Every night, when I got home, Calvin was there waiting. Then I came back to town. People started meddlin', talkin' behind my back . . . some people, that is. I've heard things--horrible things, gossip, lies. **[Throws cards down.]** Who'll take my hand?

[Leona walks by the front table. She goes off through the darkened side of the stage. A record begins to play-- "Until the Real Thing Comes Along," by Andy Kirk and the Clouds of Joy.]

RUTH: Lay Leona's hand down. Somebody'll bid for it.

MARY JANE: I'll tell you how it oughta be: my boy comes home, marks his school papers, smart as a tack! Leafs through a book or two, maybe has a good hot cup of tea, all the while your girl's there making sure of everything. He only has to look up, give a nod. That's all.

EMMA: Lie low, catch a meddler.

MARY JANE: Don't you know a man gets tired, just thinkin'?

EMMA: Well, I'm thinkin' I'm a Christian, so I can't say what's on my mind.

MARY JANE: Any other woman around here, have my boy to come home to, smart as he is? Sweet heaven, she'd be there now.

[Emma looks around for Leona.]

THEODORA: She's lyin' down, Mother.

[Emma nods, takes off her apron.]

EMMA: Now let me tell you something. **[Turns to Mary Jane.]** If you want to judge, judge me. I'm proud of my children.

MARY JANE: Proud that you cooked her husband's meals?

EMMA: Good and proud. Mary Jane, the two of us, we taught together--you and me. My daughter's a teacher.

MARY JANE: Teacher! I wish Sampson could see the way she's fixed up right now. Hair all curled and greased, dress open at the neck.

EMMA: The child's entertaining her club.

MARY JANE: Entertaining, all right. A songstress, that's what you raised. You brought her up to perform and go on.

EMMA: That's right! I brought her up to perform and go on.

MARY JANE: Emma Edwards . . .

EMMA: I brought her up to be gracious and refined, to bring a ray of hope to any gathering.

MARY JANE: Emma Edwards, I come to see if your daughter's going to do the right thing.

EMMA: My daughter's not on trial. If you want to judge, judge me.

MARY JANE: All right, I'll say it then. I heard you singing and playing over to the school. Songstress--that's what they called you! Playin' that ragtime piano, right there at the school dance.

[Emma puts her hands on her hips and squints at Mary

Jane.]

You call that Christian? I been knowin' you all my life. Why, I remember the day I saw you and Will Edwards walkin' home from school. He dared you to take your hair loose, down over by that bridge. I saw your mother come lookin' for you. Saw her pull out a switch, long green one 'bout the size of this finger. She whipped you all the way home.

EMMA: Judge me, Mary Jane. **[Emma reaches up and undoes the bun in the back of her head. She shakes her head and her long, heavy hair falls over her shoulders.]**

MARY JANE: Alright. I've seen you put on dresses all done in satin and silk, all sorts of finery, wastin' hard-earned money. They say you put on fancy clothes and shawls with fringes just to sit up in the house. When that ol' show comes to town you run off and follow 'em, up to the school. For what?

EMMA: We hid from my ma! I paid three dollars when *Shuffle Along* came to town--two nights at the old Macedonia School. Me and my chum Olivia, we dreamed--went on for days about dressing in silk. We shined our shoes with biscuits and painted our eyes just to sit and watch . . .

MARY JANE: *Shuffle Along*! **[scornfully]** *Silas Green*!

EMMA: Our cousin, the one wore tie and tails to supper, he was in all those shows that came through here. *Shuffle Along*, *Brownskin Models*, all those shows.

[Mimicking a gesture she has seen in the traveling shows, Emma brings hands up simultaneously in clockwise and counter-clockwise circles.]

MARY JANE: *Brownskin Models*? Skirts up to the neck. You call that Christian?

EMMA: I'll tell you Christian--go up yonder to St. Paul's A. M. E. Church up on Macedonia Hill. Look by the front of the church. My pappy's name is right on the cornerstone. He helped build that church.

MARY JANE: A. M. E.? African Methodist. Well, that's about the only African thing about you. Son, I said go on down to Mt. Lebanon, find a nice lookin' Baptist girl--no sirree, not him, he had to run all the way cross town . . . . A. M. E. . . . You an' your high yellow . . .

EMMA: African Methodists.

MARY JANE: I told him, I said, marry a Baptist. You and your high yellow . . .

EMMA: Now let me tell you something. Go on down to Mt. Lebanon Missionary Baptist Church. You said it--Mt. Lebanon Baptist Church. Tiptoe around the altar and climb up in the pulpit. Open up the Old Settlers' Bible. Turn to the first page. Run your fingers down the page: my grandma, Liza, my great-grandpappy, Demps; they set the first stone. Every which a way I turn--I got it on both sides. Baptist this a way, A.M.E that a way. High is right. Look up high--that's where you'll see Emma Edwards. I never made a difference between light and dark. Never made a thing about color. Why, my own pappy was the blackest man you've ever seen. My mother loved him and married him. **[Emma takes her hair and throws it over her shoulder.]**

MARY JANE: Injun hair--I can see who you come from. Well, I think your daughter's too high falutin', that's her problem.

[Mary Jane hears noise, turns to see Marietta entering the room carrying a stack of hymnals.]

EMMA: If you think my daughter's so high falutin', then why you here askin' about her? My daughter's carryin' a child, your son's child. Don't nobody care about whether your son's light or dark. I got four girls, and they all have the same father. I nursed them all, raised them all, never said, well, this one's first, this one's lighter.

[Marietta drops her stack of hymnals.]

MARY JANE: **[Mary Jane hears the noise and looks around, hoping to see Leona.]** Where's your daughter?

EMMA: Which one, Mary Jane? The real bright one? Leona? Didn't you see her walk out?

MARY JANE: The reason she's not goin' back with my boy . . .

EMMA: You're the reason.

MARY JANE: The reason she's not goin' back with my boy . . . I don't think he's the father in the first place. You heard me.

EMMA: And just who do you think the father might be, Sister Jane?

MARY JANE: You know that's Roy Murchison's child.

EMMA: Roy who?

MARY JANE: You heard me. Roy D. Murchison.

EMMA: Roy Murchison? That wayward piece of. . . Why he can't half spell his own name. Roy D. Murchison. Lord ha' mercy.

MARY JANE: Emma Edwards. Don't you take the Lord's name in vain.

EMMA: All my girls, Mary Jane, and get this straight-- every one of my girls will always know the father of her children.

MARY JANE: Dark as Calvin is? Why, that child'll be light enough to pass.

EMMA: Pass? Pass for what? Why Marietta Edwards, my own newborn, was as white as a bedsheet the day I gave birth to her. Look at how dark the child is now.

[Marietta suppresses a grin and covers her face.]

MARY JANE: There's only one thing Calvin wants.

EMMA: And what's that?

MARY JANE: He wants his gold. He wants it back.

[Stage is dark. Leona walks to spotlight. Fadeout on other lights.]

LEONA: [Holds up the chain with the ring on it.] He wants this back. Why should I give it to him? The day we ran off to get married, I wore flowers in my hair. I was teaching school out at Morning Star. And he was living down at Miss Estelle's-- that's how we met. That night after we came back from Tuskegee--never saw so many flowers--we went back to Miss Estelle's.

I didn't go out much at A & I. Me and Roy Murchison, we courted. You weren't 'lowed off campus on school nights. Had to go in groups on Saturdays. Of course I went to the formal dances.

[Leona's music starts. "Until the Real Thing Comes Along," by Andy Kirk's Orchestra.]
Wore beautiful clothes from Aunt Ellen. Everybody at school wanted to wear my clothes. I just wanted to get good grades, that's all. Be invited into the honorary.

After I finished A & I, one of the teachers over to the school came up to me, said "Calvin, you remember Calvin Barnes, good family, went to Fisk too. He's stayin' over to Miss Estelle's. Getting ready to teach at Macedonia Hill. He's a Kappa. Goes to all the dances up in Nashville?" I thought and I thought. No, I didn't know him . . . tall, a quick little smile, broad shoulders, suits straight from New York, fitted just so at the waist--neat as a band box. You should have seen us at the Elks.

I can still wear my clothes. If I go to the club dance in Pett and Doctor's basement, I'll wear one of Aunt Ellen's dresses. Won't even show. My mother-in-law says I'm carrying Roy Murchison's child. It's a lie and she knows it. One thing, I will always know the father of my children. I know it'll be a girl. I know how she'll be, not too light and not too dark, the same color all over. Of course, as soon as they find out you're expecting, you have to stop teaching. I don't know why. This saleslady uptown didn't even notice. Am I foolish, vain? Don't I have a right to be? It's my ring. Why should I give it back?

That Saturday after club meeting I put my purse down on the dresser. Tucked my gloves inside the strap. Said "Calvin, I'm going to have our child." **[Imitates man's voice.]** "A child . . . whose child? **[Mimics Calvin's laugh.]** That's no child of mine." That night I cried and cried--went running home to Mother. All right--I'm sorry-- if you're looking for a big hero--I never was that brave. Was I supposed to sit there like a dummy? If you don't whine, who'll know you're alive? If you can't stand things, don't you have to let somebody in this world know? Mary

Jane Barnes . . . [**Turns to look at women.**] she sure makes me hot. It's a good thing Papa's not here. He'd put her out.

[**Spotlight fades; bring up lights on bridge players. Music stops.**]

EMMA: My Leona never did rip and run like some girls. I sent her to Hale Dormitory at A & I. All my girls lived at Hale.

MARY JANE: You know there's something odd about a woman who waits till she's twenty-nine to marry and have a family.

EMMA: My Leona. She taught right there at Macedonia. Just like all the rest of your husband's teachers.

MARY JANE: Being principal never meant watching every move.

EMMA: Sampson Barnes does.

MARY JANE: Gettin' late. I'm a real busy woman, too busy to get all dolled up just to play Miss La Dee Da, sit up in the house and eat folks' food all day. Why, I never in my life held a card.

EMMA: Lie low, catch meddler.

MARY JANE: I'm not meddlin'. You hear me--my son wants his own.

EVA ZOE: [**Jumps up from her seat.**] A girl would have to be crazy to give up all that gold.

[**Theodora stands up and pushes Eva Zoe down.**]

MARY JANE: My boy wants his ring.

EMMA: Well, maybe he'd better come and get it.

MARY JANE: Either the ring goes back or she comes back. **[Turns to door where Leona exited. Yells loudly in direction of the door.]** My boy needs a wife waitin' for him when he comes home from the war. Either sign on with my boy or give me that ring. You heard me. Go on. Call it off, if you want to. I can't stop you. But the ring goes back.

[Lights fade.]

ACT TWO

[A record begins to play "Until the Real Thing Comes Along." The time is early Saturday evening. Normally the club meeting would be over by now, but the women are still together.]

THEODORA: Everybody oughta be back from Nashville by now. The rest of the gang'll be tippin' in. **[to Eva Zoe]** Leona sure does love that old record.

EVA ZOE: Bet you're thinking about the club dance.

THEODORA: That old song. Not for our dance.

MARIETTA: They didn't bring that boy Cordie Cheek back from Nashville.

[Music stops. Women look at Marietta.]

LEONA: **[Enters, walks to her table and steadies herself on a chair.]** I thought his trial was over.

MARIETTA: It was over, all right.

LEONA: When school let out, he came up. Said "Miss Leona, we're leavin' the country, comin' to town. I'll be at Macedonia Hill before you can say Jack Robinson. You'll be my teacher." He didn't know I wouldn't be there.

RUTH: Hair combed, shoes all shined. I can see him now.

THEODORA: You know how people talk. He'll be all right.

MARIETTA: They didn't bring him back, Theodora.

THEODORA: Listen to the superintendent. You all--Marietta's tellin' those tales again.

SAMUELLA: He went before the grand jury.

PETT MAE: The paper said they freed him on that charge of messing with a white girl.

MARIETTA: After the girl's own ma died, the pa too, Miss Tenny, the Cheek boy's mother, she raised all of 'em, the girl, her brother, all the rest of that bunch out there, cooked and cleaned, treated 'em like her own. She brought everyone of 'em into this world.

LEONA: Cordie played out there, right along with the rest of those children.

MARIETTA: I'm telling you now, and this ain't no tall tale. Mr Saul told me. They had a party on that old bridge over there.

LEONA: He was a little boy out in the country at Theta. That's where I taught him.

MARIETTA: They really had a party on that old bridge.

LEONA: I brushed his teeth, showed him how to lace his shoes. Out in the country you teach everything.

MARIETTA: Cordie Cheek's gone. I'm tellin' you now and this ain't no tale. Mr. Saul told me. They hung him on the way back from Nashville. You know, by the Murfreesboro Pike, on that old bridge that goes over the Duck River. Big crowd waitin' when they drove up with Cordie Cheek, old ones, young ones. Soon as they stopped the car . . .

[Several women stand up at their seats. Others hold

bridge hands to their chests. Leona grasps the chain at her neck.]

PETT MAE: He was a marked man.

EMMA: A man? That boy wadn't but eighteen years old.

MARIETTA: After the grand jury freed the boy, the girl's brother and his gang, they hunted him down.

EMMA: Like a pack of wild dogs.

MARIETTA: Snatched him up from over to his auntie's house in Nashville. When they turned off the road by that old bridge. . .

EMMA: Whole lot of 'em, just a waitin', 'specting to have a big party.

MARIETTA: Mr. Saul Blanton . . . he's the first to know. . . knows everything. What he told me . . . after they stopped the car. Said you shoulda seen the folks comin' out of the bushes. Said the Cheek boy tried to run off. The brother, the whole gang, they went right after him, grabbed the boy, held him down, with him screamin' and hollerin' the whole time. They kept him out there two hours, wanted the boy to write a confession--but his hands . . .

[Leona moans. Marietta holds her right hand up to the light and turns it slowly.]

they were burned so bad--he couldn't even move. Said they passed a whole lot of pistols around the crowd. Wanted everybody to have a turn. I heard they shot him close up, that's what Mr. Saul said, said you could see the powder burns, then they hung him before he died.

[Pett Mae knocks talcum powder off cards. The cars come by again, but this time they stop. A car door can be heard closing. There are footsteps, a pause, then a noise near the window. A man's voice calls through the screen door.]

MAN'S VOICE: Anybody home?

[The door opens suddenly.]

[Townsend, a large, middle-aged white man, hatless with thinning hair, is standing there wearing a deputy's badge pinned to the lapel of his open-collared shirt. He looks around the room, then scowls at the player piano.]

TOWNSEND: Y'all tryin' to hide somethin'? **[Goes over to piano and bangs the keys.]** Where'd you get this? **[He walks over to Pett Mae, looks at her dress. Goes back to the door and yells outside.]** Hey Byrd! Byrd! Come on, hurry up, they raisin' hell in here.

EMMA: And what might we do for you this fine afternoon, sir?

[Frank Byrd, the younger deputy, steps in quickly, looks around, then glares at Townsend. He is thin and wiry. Wearing a white shirt, tie and expensive gold cufflinks, he seems to be dressed for a social occasion, as though his appearance here is the result of a last-minute decision. His temporary deputy's badge is stuffed in his pocket.]

BYRD: Townsend, will you stop all that infernal yellin'?

TOWNSEND: Hey Byrd! Look here. This darkie been playin' poker for money. **[Townsend points to Pett Mae.]**

BYRD: **[Frank Byrd ignores Emma and points to Pett**

Mae nervously, then yells.] Townsend, over here's the wife of our colored doctor and that one over there, she's a colored undertaker.

TOWNSEND: Undertaker! **[Jumps, nudges Byrd, laughs, then turns away from Pett Mae.]** Lord, I'm tired. Been all over town. I was up on Main Street, heard this gunshot, like to went right through me. **[Grabs side, then goes over to piano and bangs on the keys.]** Lord, if I told my pa about this . . .

BYRD: Better send you to the doctor, Townsend.

TOWNSEND: Doctor? Well, I ain't goin'. My mammy, two my brothers, they all died of the pox. The doc, he never came out to the Hollow but once--too busy treatin' the rich folk. **[beat]** Say, you ever hear the one about the undertaker and the farmer's widow?

BYRD: Maybe we'll send you to the colored doc. He treats a heap of our folks.

TOWNSEND: A nigger? Look here, college boy.

BYRD: Townsend, like I told you, you're not in Alabama now and furthermore the name's Byrd. Byrd, that's what you call me, understand?

TOWNSEND: College boy. All slicked up. Tie, shirt shining all round the cuff. **[Holds up Byrd's arm to show cufflink.]** Like he's goin' to the Opry. How you gone play the law, dressin' up like a choir boy?

BYRD: Know where you are, Townsend? Well, do you? You're in Will Edwards' house. We don't say that in here.

[Mary Jane is outside. She appears suddenly and

54

watches quietly through the window.]

TOWNSEND: I tell you what I know--know trouble when I see it. Gamblin', sittin' up holdin' hands fulla cards. Lord, if I tole my pa about this . . . a piano. Come on y'all, it's time for Grand Ole Opry. **[Starts humming loudly.]** Ain't it, Byrd?

[Leans against tables and talks to Byrd as if women aren't there. Bumps into Pett Mae and then jumps away, feigning fear.]

BYRD: The colored doctor--fellow named B. F.--my uncle, aunt, four cousins, whole family goes down there.

TOWNSEND: He ain't no real doctor, is he, college boy? **[Goes over to piano and rubs his hands across it.]**

[Samuella raps hand on table, looks insulted.]

BYRD: They say he is, and if he isn't, I'm gonna turn you over to the undertaker, one in the white dress over there.

[They stand talking as if they are alone.]

TOWNSEND: Where? Undertaker where?

[Byrd points to Ruth.]

BYRD: Your kind . . . you don't listen, do you, Townsend?

TOWNSEND: Her? Uh, uh, no sir. **[Moves away from Ruth.]** No sir --I'm 'fraid 'a undertakers. That's bad luck, bad, bad luck and a female undertaker--a nigger--that's double, triple bad. You ever hear the one about the undertaker? Him and the widow, see, they're at the wake. . .

[Byrd pushes him away.]

TOWNSEND: Where I come from, if you see a whole lot of women livin' in a big ol' house playin' card games, strange men in and out all day and half the night, first one then the other--a piano--entertainin' they call it--a bunch of us, we get together with the Klan, ride in, and make 'em stop.

BYRD: And if they don't?

TOWNSEND: We run 'em out of town.

BYRD: Alabama style.

TOWNSEND: Go on, just try it. Start a cathouse in Farley, gamblin'-- shoot . . . The Klan, they come through one night, burn down every cathouse in Lima County. Heap o' folks, the colored, they don't understand the Klan.

[Samuella spreads her cards in front of her face.]

(to the women) Understand this! That's right! They took care a that boy. Neighbor up my way knows the girl. Whole family. Good folk. Real fine. **(to himself)** Said the law didn't do what it was 'sposed to do. Said the girl's brother had to take care of it hisself. Show all a you a thing or two.

BYRD: **[mutters]** Worse than the poorest trash.

TOWNSEND: Boy--what you say? My pa always said if you keep your ladies pure, make sure everybody else does, too . . .

BYRD: Townsend, this here's the wife of Will Edwards, takes the white sportsmen fishin'. Howdy, *Miss* Emma.

EMMA: Afternoon. **[Turns to him quickly, as if seeing him for the first time.]** Why, if it isn't young Mr. Frank,

Judge Jordan Cooper's grandbaby home from Vanderbilt.

TOWNSEND: Howdy. **[Bows in an exaggerated manner to Emma, then turns to Byrd.]** Howdy, Vandy.

EMMA: Home from law school.

TOWNSEND: Vandy!

BYRD: Howdy, Aunt Emma. Don't mind him. I know you folks. Been knowing you since I was a little boy.

EMMA: Yes sir. **[Bows slightly, shifts feet a little.]**

TOWNSEND: They got a bunch of us to come here, take care of things. 'Cause a all the trouble that boy caused.

EMMA: We wouldn't be causing any trouble. **[Smiles beatifically.]**

TOWNSEND: Well, we ain't lookin' for none either. You the ones started all this mess. We been told to go to every colored in town. Collect all the guns.

EMMA: Why sir . . .

BYRD: Emma, we know Will has a gun. **[Turns to Townsend.]** Best damn guide around. Ask anybody.

TOWNSEND: Guide? Vandy, what you know about guidin'? Ain't hardly used a razor.

BYRD: If you go out with him, Townsend, you can't drink or swear. He's got rules--not one bird over the limit. We were out on the Duck River one day, Mr. Will Edwards was paddlin' the boat with one hand, reached up, shot a duck out of the air with the other. And you know, the water didn't even move.

[Townsend laughs and moves closer.]

Next time we go, I'll call you. Only five dollars a man for the whole day.

[Townsend jerks away angrily.]

[Eva Zoe sees Mary Jane watching, points at the window.]

EVA ZOE: [loudly] Miss Mary Jane . . . [covers her mouth]

[Theodora pushes her down in her seat. Townsend whips around and hears a noise at the window. Mary Jane hides. He walks over and looks out the window.]

TOWNSEND: We been up and down the hill, all over Mink Slide, all the way to the bottom. Got every gun. Any you niggers mess with me. Any your boys act up again, we got somethin' for 'em.

[Pett Mae and Ruth huddle around Leona, murmuring words of comfort. Townsend sits down at their table. Pett Mae starts to chatter nervously.] You, [Points at Pett.] the doc's wife, the one gon' sew me up, shut your mouth.

[Pett Mae continues to chatter.]

I said shut your mouth! Damn it, I said shut up.

[Looks at Byrd and then at Pett Mae. Townsend slaps his knee. Pett Mae starts to cry. Leona stares at Pett Mae unbelievingly, then covers face with hands.]

Do I have to tell you again?

BYRD: Told my pa, Aunt Emma. Said don't go pickin' up any old piece of trash. Aunt Emma, we know Mr. Will's got a gun. We're going to Saul Blanton's house up the street. **[to Townsend]** Bootlegger's bound to keep guns in the house. Cock fights, gamblin' half the night. Got to keep order over all that. Emma, when we come back, we want that gun.

[Mary Jane appears at the window again, then rushes away, Townsend and Byrd walk toward door.]

TOWNSEND: We goin' up to that bootlegger. Me and Vandy gon' have us a party all night.

BYRD: Gamblin'? Klan hear that, they might not want you--run you out of Farley. **[Goes over to piano bench and picks up hat.]** Sorry, Townsend, I'm busy.

TOWNSEND: Bet you are, school boy. I bet you are.

[Townsend and Byrd exit.]

MARIETTA: Half the white folks in town buy their liquor from Saul Blanton. 'Course he bootlegs something stronger than that. **[She stands by the door, looking out.]** Well, I 'spect they'll be comin' back down here t'rectly--Byrd and his deputy.

THEODORA: Deputy, my foot.

RUTH: **[Holds Pett Mae's hand, tries to comfort her.]** Who in the world sent for that old deputy showed up here with Frank Byrd? Never seen hide nor hair of him in my life.

MARIETTA: **[Looks out window.]** No tellin'. They line 'em up, hand 'em a gun and a badge. Reckon that's all the schoolin' they need.

[As the women talk, Emma stares at the window. She pats her foot angrily.]

LEONA: Poor little Pett Mae. Are you scared? They didn't hurt you, did they? Did they, Pett honey?

PETT MAE: Let's see. I went up town, paid the light bill. Did I remember to pick up that dress from Gordon's? I'll have Doctor's helper go by there this evening.

EVA ZOE: College of Physicians and Surgeons--that's where Doctor went, didn't he, Pett?

SAMUELLA: A real doctor--the nerve.

PETT MAE: **[Gives Ruth a reassuring hug.]** Ol' Samuella. Always rufflin' up.

THEODORA: What's a cathouse?

[Emma glares at Theodora. Stands with hands on hips. Samuella coughs. There is a long silence.]

SAMUELLA: **[Rises from her seat.]** Ladies, I speak to you as your parliamentarian. We will not dignify the various and sundry vulgar comments made in our presence.

EVA ZOE: Amen.

THEODORA: If that old man's a deputy, my little schoolchildren might as well be.

MARIETTA: Don't matter what you think. If he puts that gun to your head you'll be gone just the same.

[Emma walks to spotlight. Fadeout on other lights. Emma addresses audience]

EMMA: [**Alternates between surly tone for the deputy and gracious manner for Emma herself.**] "What you all doin' up there playin' poker for money?" [**graciously**] "Why sir, we wouldn't be doing a thing like that."

You know I always wanted to be on the stage. Judge Cooper's grandbaby couldn't match that. My mother always said "Lie low, catch meddler." That's "lie low, catch a meddler." The law's known for putting its nose in other folks' business. One night they drove right up to the house. Said "What you darkies doin' up there on that porch?" I said, "Why, sir, we're just out getting a spot of evening air." So they said to me, "Well, you better get on in the house." And I said "Why sir, this is just Emma Edwards up here on the porch with her family." And he says "Will Edwards' wife? Doggone." So I said, "Why, yes sir." And off he drove.

You know I always wanted to be on the stage. I'm a performin' woman. When I was comin' up church folks weren't allowed to sing and go on for a living. Me and my chum Olivia, we performed over to the old Macedonia school. I used to be the end man for the minstrel show. Oh, I was something in my time. I walked for the cake. [**Demonstrates step.**] Did the real Charleston--not the way they try to do it now. Roll your eyes if you want to, but I've been goin' to church on Sunday and to the meeting of the Phyllis Wheatley Circle and to my lodge longer than I care to remember. You can't fault Emma Edwards there. After I was grown, Mama couldn't say a thing. I would get up on the stage and do the Charleston. Played the piano for all my girls. For every last one of their dances, Right over there. At old Macedonia school. [**Points to corner. Sings out loud, first line of song only.**] "There'll be a Hot Time in the Old Town Tonight." All the songs didn't go fast, either. Sometimes I'd go slow

[Moves slowly, gesturing with hands, sings to waltz time first few lines of "I'm Just Wild About Harry." Continue instrumental of "I'm Just Wild About Harry" up and under.]

I sang and played one night till Will Harold came up and got me, that's his real name, William Harold Edwards, always called him Will, said "Woman, come from over there--they can hear you singin' all the way to Nashville." Will Edwards wodden't the only one tried to boss me. When my girls start tryin' to tell me what to do, I just tell them "Darlin', why your mother's forgotten more than you'll ever know."

I've got something waitin' for that ol' deputy and Byrd too! I'm used to people talkin'. Just let 'em talk. Talk themselves out. Won't change my mind. Furthermore, won't get 'em anywhere, either. If I had to count the times folks've stopped here and stayed for dinner . . . 'bout half the town. I remember the time I baked chicken, made teeniny little rolls, real light and that charlotte russe. Wish I had some teeniny little rolls about now. I never have closed my door to folks, specially meddlers. Meddlers, they're real sly--you won't catch one--don't even say hello when they pass unless they've got a reason. I've never fought with one, don't get mad either. I just let them talk, then I strut around, sing a little, smile and send them on their way--they're halfway down the road before they figure anything's wrong. I never have closed my door--specially to meddlers.

[Continue music to end. Music fades. Spotlight fades. Bring up lights on the women. It's getting dark outside. None of the women have left, although the club meeting has been over for some time. As the women circulate around the room, they seem relaxed and sociable. An atmosphere of underlying tension, however, has been created by the news of Cordie Cheek's lynching.]

THEODORA: Mother sure loves to perform.

[Emma eyes Theodora sheepishly. Emma sits still, not moving; thoughtful pose. Marietta enters, stepping lightly. She goes over to the phone on the wall and places a call.]

MARIETTA: **[Talks for a minute quietly.]** Yes sir, Mr. Saul. I thank you kindly. **[Hangs up phone, turns to Emma and women.]** Well, Mr. Saul says he's been entertaining Frank Byrd and his deputy.

PETT MAE: If anybody can cut a rug, it's ol' Saul.

[Leona enters room. Sits down in chair. No music.]

RUTH: How you feelin', Leona?

LEONA: I'll pass, I guess.

RUTH: It's the weather. When I was carryin' Gene, got so bad one night, had to sleep out on the porch. **[Fans herself.]**

LEONA: I keep thinkin' about Cordie Cheek. That child. I taught that child three years. . . seems like I been knowin' him all my life. Mother, I can't help myself.

EMMA: Help yourself! Help yourself to bed. That's all you need to do right now.

LEONA: It's a good thing Calvin's not here. Hot as he is, they'd have the whole lot of us up to the courthouse. We'd all be on trial.

[Theodora looks uncomfortable. Emma shakes her head and closes her eyes as if to cancel out Leona's words.]

RUTH: Look at Mama Emma.

PETT MAE: She's not about to let them mess with her.

EVA ZOE: Not Mama Emma.

[Theodora is looking off into space, trying not to listen to the conversation. Leona is trying to get her attention. Emma is still deep in thought.]

LEONA: **[Holds up satin pillow cover, turns to Theodora.]** Theodora. Theodora, every time I see this, I start thinking about Calvin. And my mother-in-law . . . Mary Jane Barnes. . . I was in the other room, but I could hear every word she said. Every word!

THEODORA: I can feel one of my headaches comin' on. Don't start all that stuff just when I'm getting ready for California.

PETT MAE: Now Theodora, that's no way to talk about your own.

LEONA: I'm trying, Theodora. I'm trying.

RUTH: Mary Jane's as bad as the law.

PETT MAE: That bird's after one of Emma Edwards' high-yellow daughters. **[Looks at Leona with a mischievous smile and touches handkerchief to her face.]**

MARIETTA: I know one thing--I sure don't have time to go round worryin' about what shade a brown I am. I'll tell you that right now.

LEONA: If I'd lived that long I'd know better than to go on like that.

EMMA: How long?

LEONA: As long as Mary Jane Barnes.

EMMA: Many an old bird shat in the nest.

[All the women laugh except Samuella, who slides down in her seat.]

Go on back to bed, Leona. Nothin' for you to do runnin' around here.

LEONA: You all won't let me do a thing. I'm older than Theodora. You let her go off to California, and she's only 22 years old. Just got her teaching certificate last June. Theodora goes everywhere.

EMMA: Theodora's not the one going to have a child. I don't have to tell you that. Now Leona darling, you know you're just a baby to me. That's all you'll ever be to your mother.

LEONA: Mother, I've been teaching almost eight years. I can take care of myself.

EMMA: You think I'd let Theodora go runnin' off to California by herself if her husband wasn't out there in the army?

THEODORA: Mother, Willie C.'ll be out there waiting, the oldest sister I got. You know she's grown.

EMMA: That's right, waiting--where's Willie C. gonna be on that long train ride out yonder? No tellin' what's out there. How long they say it was?

["Take the A-Train" up and under.]

PETT MAE: Six days.

THEODORA: I don't have to go by myself.

EMMA: You don't have to go at all.

THEODORA: Leona could go with me.

[Music stops.]

EMMA: Leona?

THEODORA: Leona--me and Leona--could make the trip together.

EMMA: Leona who? Leona's having a child this month. How's Leona going all the way out to California?

RUTH: Leona? Her insides never would take a trip like that. After a baby it takes months to get yourself straightened out.

SAMUELLA: Ladies, please! We're at club meeting.

MARIETTA: Sometimes you mess yourself up for life.

RUTH: Pett?

EVA ZOE: Pett girl . . .

RUTH: Bring on the major-domo.

PETT MAE: Doctor wouldn't have it. A train trip . . .

EVA ZOE: In the colored car!

SAMUELLA: Mopped and cleaned once a year!

PETT MAE: A train trip could start the worst hemorrhaging. I knew of this one girl . . . she started right on the train. And it's even worse for the baby.

SAMUELLA: If my mother could hear this . . .

THEODORA: Well, that's not what they say now.

PETT MAE: They? Who's "they"?

THEODORA: Pett, it's all the latest.

EVA ZOE: Listen to the expert.

MARIETTA: Can't even stand the sight of blood.

THEODORA: Hush, Marietta! Everybody up at Meharry's heard it.

MARIETTA: Up at Meharry. Girl won't even clean a chicken. Fainted only time she ever tried it, talkin' about Meharry.

THEODORA: Why, I've heard of women getting up and walking the next day. Eating whatever they want.

EVA ZOE: Leona can do that now.

[Women laugh.]

PETT MAE: With her stomach all torn up, why it would be a crime. If Doctor . . . a woman could drive herself half-crazy carryin' on that way. Why, our Leona never would recover.

[Ruth comforts Pett. Samuella nods her head repeatedly. Marietta listens to the conversation from the doorway near the piano; she continues to look towards the

front door at frequent intervals.]

THEODORA: Maybe she could leave the baby here, start a new life.

[Leona does not respond.]

EMMA: **[to Theodora]** A new life? Now let me tell you something, Theodora Edwards Nicholson, and you get this straight--no daughter of mine's gonna leave a child and go runnin' off somewhere.

THEODORA: Oh mother, it's nothing like that.

LEONA: The whole town'll be talkin'.

EMMA: The whole town's already talkin'.

LEONA: Folks say . . .

EMMA: What folks? Don't tell me about "folks."

LEONA: They say raising a baby without a father . . .

[Samuella's hands fly up to her mouth.]

EMMA: Who's "they"? You always talkin' about "they." Girl, if you have to go runnin' in every direction every time this one says that way and the other says this way, you'll be runnin' all your life. They . . . who's "they?" Nice-nasty, that's what it is. As long as I can remember, Leona, I've been tellin' you, if you do what everybody says just to be doing it, and then you turn your nose up when things get a little dirty even if it's for a good reason, you'll be an old bird up in a nest and you still won't know which way to turn--you won't know which way's right and which way's wrong. You remember what I called it--I said "nice-nasty."

You hold your head up, Leona Edwards, even if you're the only one who thinks you ought to, even if the whole town's preachin' and moanin'.

LEONA: Sometimes they won't hire you back teaching after you have a baby.

EMMA: My daughter wouldn't worry about that, even if she had to wash and iron--day and night.

THEODORA: Now, Mother, Leona's a school teacher. She shouldn't . . .

EMMA: **[Pats her foot up and down to her own words, speaks loudly to drown out Theodora.]** And never see that child awake. She'd work her fingers to the bone.

LEONA: Mother, I don't know if I can do it on my own.

EMMA: You're Emma Edwards' daughter. You're not on your own--and don't you forget it.

LEONA: What about Miss Mary Jane?

EMMA: What about her? No use goin' on over a whole lot of things you can't change. Life wasn't meant to fit your purpose, or anybody else's, for that matter.

THEODORA: Maybe Leona can get some money from the Thatchers.

MARIETTA: There you all go, talking about that mess again.

EMMA: Don't you talk about your forefathers, young lady. Now, you listen to me, my mama was John Thatcher's own daughter . . . Why I remember, I wodden't but so high. My ma would take me down to the courthouse, Saturday after Saturday.

MARIETTA: Used to say Fridays.

EMMA: Woman, don't you know I was a school girl writing out lessons all day Friday? Don't you get ol' Injun riled up. Saturday after Saturday we'd go up the stairs, way up top of the courthouse, great big desk, a white man, long silver hair, fell in a wave. He'd reach in his pocket like so,

[Emma beckons. Marietta leans over, looks in Emma's apron pocket and smiles.]

say "Ellen, here take this for the children, buy the little ones some shoes." My ma, she never said one word. After a while, I just couldn't stand it. One morning, bright and early we were halfway down the stairs . . . I turned round, looked back up, said "Ma, who was that old white man?" She looked down at me. Like so: "Why Emma darling, that old white man was your own uncle, Judge Hamilton Thatcher."

MARIETTA: Next thing you know she'll have her old Injun grandpa struttin' right up to the courthouse.

EMMA: Look at you. Injun yourself.

LEONA: Marietta, don't you sass now.

EMMA: She always did sass me. Sasses her own ma. But I'll tell you darkies one thing. Half the town's sittin' on Emma Edwards' land.

LEONA: The biggest plantation in middle Tennessee.

MARIETTA: Used to be the biggest. They're not that grand anymore.

EMMA: Why, they sent a car out to get me for every one of their funerals.

[Cars go by.]

MARIETTA: Ain't seen them since you graduated.

[Marietta walks to the door and looks out.]

(to herself) And she won't either.

[Marietta opens the door. Mary Jane rushes in, pushing past Marietta.]

EVA ZOE: Miss Mary Jane! (sits quickly)

MARY JANE: Cars runnin' up and down the street. Keeping a woman on foot from going back to her own house. Couldn't get home. Had to walk all the way back up the hill.

EMMA: The law's out everywhere these days.

MARY JANE: Well, I don't want them asking me--trying to find out where I'm going. They'll pay for killing Cordie Cheek. When people take things that don't belong to them, they ought to pay.

EMMA: The law knows what they did.

MARY JANE: When somebody takes somethin' . . . Better not lay a hand on my boy.

LEONA: You think they'll hurt Calvin? (Starts to cry.) Mother, I swear I think I'm 'bout to pass out.

RUTH: Poor child, must be the flu.

LEONA: Poor Calvin . . .

EVA ZOE: Don't get your pretty dress all rumpled, Leona. Press the lace down around the collar.

[Leona carefully follows Eva Zoe's instructions.]

There, that's better. Now stand up and smooth your skirt.

[Leona stands up, then collapses into the chair.]

EMMA: Marietta--Look in yonder in that cabinet behind the stove. Fetch me that bottle of tonic. Get a move on.

LEONA: Mother, I can feel it coming on. This teeniny little pain, started right here. It's going all the way up my arm.

EMMA: [to Marietta] Tie an assifidity bag around her neck. [softly] Rest yourself, Mary Jane.

MARY JANE: When somebody takes something that doesn't belong to them in the first place, you never forget.

[Emma sits on edge of straight-backed chair, silently rocking back and forth, staring straight ahead.]

I had to come back. I wodden't a been nothin' out there by myself. Not that I was leaving the whole thing for good. I planned to come back to East Hill anyway. My boy…

LEONA: [Starts walking around.] Calvin. As hot as he is, if he gets in a fight over there, starts speaking his mind, they'll throw him right in jail. He better stay out of trouble.

[Mary Jane looks on. Moves closer to Leona.]

Marietta, Marietta, you gettin' ready to serve that vanilla cream and a little piece of Miss Estelle's cake?

[Marietta comes out carrying a bottle and a teaspoon. After some coaxing, she gets Leona to sit down and open her mouth. Still looking at Leona, Mary Jane pulls up a chair and accidentally bangs into the table as she sits down.]

EMMA: Mary Jane, was that you, or the chair broke?

[The women are fanning Leona.]

MARY JANE: My feet--my whole body's 'bout to give way. My throat's dry as that wind out there. Took all I had to come back here. **[Looks startled, as if finally realizing what has happened.]** I was driven back. All because of what they did to that boy on the way back from Nashville. Bunch of thieves. They're trying to blame us all. I circled back, turned all the way around; my mind's just a spinnin' and spinnin'. But I want you to know I didn't forget. I'm still gonna get it back. I still want my ring.

[No one responds. Finally Theodora heaves a dejected sigh.]

THEODORA: Some people sure do have a lot of nerve.

EMMA: Folks need to rest. Walked all the way up East Hill--a glass of water for our guest.

[Emma steps forward and motions to Theodora. Theodora gets up and hands Mary Jane Barnes a glass of water. Women murmur in unison. Mary Jane watches from her chair.]

Give this traveler, weary that she might be, a drink of water.

[Women murmur again. Room darkens a little. then up

on Mary Jane. She takes a sip of water, sits the glass down and walks to the spotlight.]

MARY JANE: Just to think, white folks, coming in here this time a night, one dressed half-a-step better than a ditch digger fixing to go to town. They march in here and see the daughters of the founders playing cards and carrying on! Wearing enough paint to make a clown blush! If they'd just cut out that high-falutin' A.M.E. mess. Lend me half an ear. Those fools saw the likes of Emma Edwards, line helped found Mt. Lebanon Baptist dancing and singing, dressed up like so. Her whole clan playing cards like some two-bit bunch of uneducated, unwashed heathens! And that Leona, sitting over there sobbing and moaning, looking to turn my grandchild into an illegitimate . . . **[Trails off.]** You mark my words. The white folks'll carry this little cameo back home with them. Pass it around from now till doomsday. Even if Sampson Barnes never missed a day of church and walks upright, straight enough to give a strong man back problems, even if Mt. Lebanon Baptist is the most scripturally sound congregation in all of Delphi, even if my Calvin graduated high school before most of those white folks graduated from diapers--won't matter. They'll leave here remembering this cabaret of cards. That's what they'll remember when they think of the Negro. Talking back. Struttin' around in front of white folks. Acting real uppity. Will Edwards' wife? Will Edwards' widow. That's what she'll be!

[Lights up on Mary Jane and the women. Laughing and talking can be heard outside the house. Men's voices are heard. A voice calls out at the screen door.]

VOICE: Sheriff's deputy.

[Theodora goes to the door. Ushers in Townsend. He is red-faced. Walks up to Theodora. Room becomes

darker. Lights down, then gradually up.]

TOWNSEND: Think college boy's tired of me. **[staggering drunk]** I think he's looking for hisself a little starlet. **[Leans over Theodora.]**

MARY JANE: Well, he better keep lookin'.

TOWNSEND: **(to Mary Jane)** You wanna know somethin'? There's a law against talkin' back. **[Turns to Theodora again.]** Ain't I seen you somewhere before?--That's right. Somethin' at the picture show. Yeah, you look real familiar. **[Scratches his head again. Theodora's expression freezes. Deputy looks around. Surveys women sitting at table.]** Where's the gun?

EMMA: I looked, sir. I looked high and low. **[Exaggerates, waving hands and feigning bewilderment.]** I do believe Will took all his guns, sir. He's gone off hunting with the colored doctors from Meharry--and with President Hale.

TOWNSEND: President who?

EMMA: Yes sir, President Hale from A & I. A & I, sir. That's the colored college up at Nashville.

TOWNSEND: Hale--hell!

[Theodora smiles, covers mouth with hand. Women turn faces down to hide laughter. Townsend looks at women, then starts to stagger.]

Do you or do you not have a gun? That's what Reilly P. Townsend wants to know.

[Marietta steps forward. Stands next to Theodora.]

EMMA: I'm doin' poorly right now.

TOWNSEND: You keep this up, they gon' close you down.

EMMA: And my daughter . . . **[Gestures to the left and to the right at all the women in the room. Townsend follows her as she gestures. He staggers, then stands erect.]** You know, she ain't quite . . . well. Her Pa ain't here and her husband's off to war. My daughter, she ain't well, you know. She's pinin' away for her soldier boy. Will's gone off hunting with the colored doctors from Nashville. And where is young Mr. Frank, Judge Cooper's grandbaby? Young Mr. Frank, Judge Cooper's grandboy, home from school.

TOWNSEND: The grandbaby's held up down there at Blanton's house. Sittin' over in a corner like he's too good or somethin'. Saturday night. Damned if that Blanton don't have everything made and put in a bottle. He sure does know how to make a fella feel at home. Never mind the college boy. I'm the law around here now.

[Mary Jane stands up, puts her hands on her hips.]

EMMA: Will's gone off hunting, sir . . .

[Women huddle in a corner.]

with all his colored gentlemen from Nashville.

TOWNSEND: I heard that already. "Gents," huh? Ain't you never heard of hospitality? Hell, it's the middle of July. This ain't the North Pole. Fella don't mind a woman puttin' on the dog. You, the one gon' operate, you goin' down the street.

[Pett Mae holds onto her chair. Townsend grabs Pett

Mae and shoves her toward the door.]

When we git through with your boys…gon' need a undertaker too.

[Points to Ruth.]

MARY JANE: When somebody takes something that's not
theirs in the first place, they ought to be tried. They ought
to pay.

TOWNSEND: **[Pulls Mary Jane closer.]**What's wrong
with this darkie? She crazy or somethin'?

**[Mary Jane turns away from deputy, grabs Emma's
dress and leans against her.]**

EMMA: **[Emma touches Mary Jane's shoulder, turns to
deputy.]** We're all doin' poorly right now. **[to Mary Jane]**
Bless your heart, Mary Jane. **[to Townsend]** You know
how a woman is when she wants her own. **[to Mary Jane]**
That boy of yours worked from sun up to sun down, till his
legs gave way under him.

**[Mary Jane looks skeptically at Emma. Emma reaches
toward her.]**

All to give my girl that stone. I can see it shining . . . all the
way over here. Great big pretty stone.

**[Townsend strains and stretches to look across the
room.]**

MARY JANE: All the way over here. **[Points to the palm
of her hand and laughs knowingly.]**

EMMA: You knew I'd come around.

MARY JANE: So, you finally took to using that head your Maker put up on your shoulders. Well, well, it's about time. **[to the women]** She's seen the light.

EMMA: Strong light. Almost blinds my eyes.

MARY JANE: **[to the women]** She can see good when she wants to, **[Laughs, nudges Eva Zoe.]** can't she?

EMMA: Your boy worked his fingers to the bone to give my girl that gold. Leona's got your ring and bless the Pete, you're sick and tired of goin' on about it.

[Townsend perks up when he hears about the jewelry.]

I know what you want--everybody in town's heard you-- you want your ring. You want it back.

MARY JANE: All of it. Anything to give my boy his own. Lord, I love that boy. I'd wear rags to church, anything to give that boy his own.

LEONA: He's gone!

[Townsend goes over to Leona and looks her over carefully. She clasps her necklace to her.]

[Mary Jane struts over to Leona, ignoring Townsend.]

MARY JANE: When somebody takes something that's not theirs in the first place . . .

[Townsend wheels around angrily, assuming that Mary Jane is speaking to him.]

EMMA: **[to Townsend]** You know she's just a heartbroken woman goin' on about our folks' foolishness.

TOWNSEND: Good thing she ain't talkin' 'bout a white man.

EMMA: Mary Jane, don't bother this fine gentleman with all our mess. Thank Mr. Townsend for all his protection.

MARY JANE: **[Glares at Townsend.]** One of these days, if that Saul Blanton keeps up all this carryin' on, they gonna pack him up and run him outta Delphi on a rail.

EMMA: **[Quickly turns to the deputy and begins to walk towards door. Mary Jane follows her.]** And all your help and great concern. But you know that Frank Byrd's just a college boy. He's liable to get into deep trouble what with all the rowdies and unpredictables Blanton lets in down there.

MARY JANE: They oughta run him out of town this very hour.

TOWNSEND: If there's any runnin' to do, Reilly Townsend gonna do it, you hear?

EMMA: Have mercy, have mercy! All this runnin' around, folks up to Blanton's all night, raisin' cain, got the poor woman half-sick. That's the truth, sir.

TOWNSEND: Runnin'--I'll run it. Gotta mind to call my boys: "Git on down here and take care of all of you."

EMMA: Run, Mr. Townsend! Go on--you need to head up there and deal with all that carryin' on. Lord knows young Mr. Frank needs you more than we do. All those folks from out of town roamin' around, keepin' up the devil all night, cockfightin' and who knows what all.

TOWNSEND: **[Looks at Emma and grins. Hesitates for**

a minute, then walks swiftly toward door. Stops, turns around. Leans over to piano. Bangs a little.] Been a long time since I felt so good. Bring on the Opry. It's Saturday night. **[Goes over to stacks of boxes containing piano rolls. Picks up one of the rolls.]** This a player piano?

EMMA: You're right again, Mr. Townsend.

TOWNSEND: I got business. Ain't got all night, you hear?

EMMA: Sure 'nough. You need to help the boy out, give the child some peace of mind. Things go on down there at Saul Blanton's folks never dreamed of in Farley.

[Emma guides Townsend towards the door. Marietta follows behind.]

TOWNSEND: Soon as I go back to Blanton's and play wet nurse to the college boy, I'll be back. You hear?

[Emma opens door and ushers Townsend out. When the deputy goes out, Marietta falls against the door in relief. For a moment, everyone is still. When Emma returns, the room fills with talking and strained laughter, expressing both mourning and relief.]

SAMUELLA: The nerve of that man.

MARIETTA: White folks think we can't own pianos.

[Emma looks on innocently, then turns away grinning, as if she is hiding a secret.]

Lord have mercy, look at Mother.

PETT MAE: **[Admiringly imitates Emma; holds hand-**

kerchief to her mouth.] "All those rowdies and unpredict-able, folks from out of town, keepin' up the devil half the night . . . "

RUTH: Mamma Emma, you plum forgot that old deputy's from out of town too.

EMMA: Darling, you know your mother knows that.

THEODORA: Mother, you ought to be shot--Will Edwards huntin' in the middle of July!

LEONA: Mother, I thought you told us Papa went fishin'.

PETT MAE: With Doctor's good old buddies from Me-harry.

MARIETTA: Might as well ask her 'bout the guns Papa left in the cellar when he went off fishing with the doctors from Meharry. Go on.

EMMA: Meddler! Thought she was out there listening to the Opry.

MARIETTA: And while you're on it, ask her about that old mahogany cabinet with the double lock. See if she'll show you that key stuffed in her apron pocket.

[Emma pretends to ignore Marietta and begins fussing with her hair.]

EMMA: That Marietta Edwards sure is one nosy child. Wonder she's got time to bother other folks so much. Better tend to her own messy self. Find all those Sunday School books she's been lookin' for all week.

MARIETTA: Go on, ask her.

PETT MAE: Not while that old deputy's down the street.

EMMA: That ol' meddler? I sent him on his way.

LEONA: Mother sure does like to perform.

RUTH: Mama Emma, it sure is too bad you couldn't have been in the traveling shows.

EMMA: Mama Emma's danced and sang all she wants to, darling. Your Mama Emma has lived her life.

THEODORA: Oh Mother, you'll be here after I'm dead and gone.

MARY JANE: **[Mary Jane has been sitting in the corner with her hands folded. She stands up, a determined look on her face.]** I'll be goin' now.

RUTH: Save me and Gene a seat at sunrise service, like you always do.

MARY JANE: **[Waves women away.]** And if you don't mind, I'll take my diamond. Got to be seein' about my supper. **[Mary Jane waits, but Emma does not respond.]** I said, I'll be taking my ring. **[Mary Jane pats the palm of her hand.]**Right here, if you please.

[Leona folds her arms.]

EMMA: Mary Jane, you oughta know I was just performin' for that old deputy.

MARY JANE: Performin' or not, the ring's mine.

EMMA: Sister Jane, you oughta know by now, that ring's not mine to give away. Never has been.

MARY JANE: I'll call the law down here right now.

EMMA: The old deputy mighta come to your aid, but he won't be back this night. When Marietta called Saul Blanton on the phone, said the law's on the way, I know Saul was waitin' when they got there. We've dealt with the law up here on East Hill many a day.

MARY JANE: You mighta dealt with the law, but you won't put me off.

[Emma grabs her hair and brings it forward over her shoulder.]

Your girl can come back, but she'll have to mind her manners, do for my boy the way she ought to.

LEONA: **[Gets up and gets the broom, starts to sweeping.]** Miss Mary Jane . . .

MARY JANE: Lay a fresh doily behind his head every evening--do whatever.

LEONA: **[Continues sweeping.]** There's a thing or two . . .

MARY JANE: Buttermilk dumplings rolled *this* thin, summer peaches, the kind I put up.

LEONA: And *if* I do go back, I don't wanna hear a thing about Roy Murchison!

[Theodora grabs the broom and guides Leona to a chair.]

I've lost one boy already, and I'm not about to lose Calvin. Miss Mary Jane, I'm stayin' right here till Calvin comes back from the war, and when he does, we're going to raise the baby right here in Delphi. That ring belongs to me and I'm keeping it. When something belongs to you, you have a right to keep it.

EMMA: **[Grabs Mary Jane by the arm.]** You're welcome here, Mary Jane, always will be.

[Motions to Marietta to bring over a chair. Mary Jane picks up chair and carries chair over to Leona and sits down next to her. Leona stares straight at Mary Jane]

LEONA: And I never messed around with Roy Murchison. You hear me? We went to the dances. That was in college up at A and I. And that's all. If I hear anything about that again . . .

[Leona rushes over to Mary Jane and holds on to her. Mary Jane doesn't move away.]

EMMA: We're not about to put anybody out. **[Looks at Ruth.]** I guess Cordie Cheeks' mother'll be coming to see you about the wake. She'll be picking out the suit.

PETT MAE: My own pappy wore the loveliest shade of blue.

LEONA: He'll look fine in his suit. He'll look fine, won't he, Ruth?

RUTH: A young boy's suit--I'll be going to see his ma. . .

LEONA: Miss Tenny.

RUTH: Sometime this evening.

[Emma starts to arrange her hair. She reaches in her apron pocket and takes out a few hair pins. Taking out

one pin at a time, she slowly pins her hair up at the top of her head.]

PETT MAE: Look who's gettin' fixed up.

MARIETTA: Mother's gone and found herself a party.

EVA ZOE: Where's the party, Mama Emma? Up there at Saul Blanton's?

EMMA: Never you mind about a party . . . I'll party you.

[Women laugh nervously. A few of them absentmindedly begin to arrange their hair and clothes as if preparing for the evening. Emma takes off her apron and throws it on the sofa, then smooths out her dress. She reaches in her pocket for another pin and puts in her hair. Mary Jane smooths her skirt and adjusts the collar of her dress.]

SAMUELLA: Look at Mother Emma dressing up.

EVA ZOE: Remember, Mama Emma, when you used to get all fixed up and play for our high school dance?

THEODORA: Mother doesn't need a party to get dressed up and step out.

MARIETTA: She never did.

LEONA: She'll start gettin' ready at the drop of a hat.

RUTH: Theodora, Eva Zoe, Sam, all you all . . . **[Ruth struggles to stand.]** I've got a body to pick up.

PETT MAE: The law's acting real ugly tonight.

THEODORA: I wouldn't set foot out there if you paid me.

[Emma walks to the door and opens it slightly--starts out.]

RUTH: Where you goin', Mama Emma?

EMMA: **[Addresses women.]** Why, I remember one night I put on everything I owned. Shawls, everything. Will said, "Lord have mercy, Emma, where you think you're going?" I turned around just like this, said "Just going out to look at the stars."

[Leona goes to the bedroom. She returns holding a soft peach crepe dress to her body. She seems to be deep in thought, then turns towards Emma.]

EMMA: **[Walks over to a chair and picks up a shawl.]** It's dark now . . . a beautiful night and the stars are all out. I guess I'll go out on the porch. The stars'll be out right about now.

[Ruth struggles, stands up and walks a few steps toward the door. Emma walks out the door while Mary Jane and the women watch.]

[Stage is dark. Spotlight on Marietta.]

MARIETTA: I don't know why things had to turn out the way they did with Cordie Cheek. God tests your faith. No point in trying to talk about how things could have been different. I just have to believe that.

Leona's been goin' on and on about Miss Mary Jane. If that's all she's got to worry about, she's done pretty well, I'd say.

I try to be real quiet, real nice and not worry folks with a whole lot of mess. When Mother starts that talk about the Thatchers, I just let her go right on. Don't say a word. Makes me no never mind.

Let other folks live in peace. That's all I know to say. Leave other folks alone. I try to help when I can, otherwise I leave them alone.

Like I said, I don't know why things had to turn out the way they did with Cordie Cheek. Folks'll go on for days, doin' a whole lot of whoopin' and hollerin'. But it won't amount to much. Saul Blanton. They think he's just a performer. Somebody to laugh at, a gambler, a bootlegger, just somebody out for money. They come runnin' through here, all the time lookin' for this old gun and that one. Saul Blanton can get a hundred guns from Chicago, just like that. Now I don't believe in gamblin' . . . That's how Saul Blanton got rich, that and bootleggin'. But sometimes you gotta fight evil with evil. They take us for a bunch of fools. They think they know where all the guns are?

Like I said, I don't approve of gamblin'--or guns either--but I don't judge people. I hope it never comes to guns--but if it does, they'll be pullin' the white folks out of the Duck River, buryin' them at night. Folks'll be on the roofs down in the Bottom, on top of Ruth and Jim's business, Saul Blanton's barber shop, Curtis's cafeteria, the Elks' lodge, with rifles aimed, just a waitin'. And when they come through--

They're busy lookin' for one gun. Time may come. I ain't sayin' it will come, but I'm tellin' you . . . Saul Blanton can get guns from Chicago any time he wants.

Now I hope it never comes to that--but the Lord works in mysterious ways. Folks may not believe this, but the whole world's lookin' right here. If you think what we say don't count, just watch. I'm not sayin' I'd fight, but we're going to get justice sometime. We're gonna get it, sure as night and day.

[Spotlight fades slowly.]

THE END

How I Came to Write *The Bridge Party*

I grew up in the South of legal segregation and illegal but almost always unpunished violence against African Americans. There was, nevertheless, something compelling and satisfying about the way of life of my family and their community, an indefinable quality that I tried to evoke in my play *The Bridge Party*. What was that something? Why is it that some of my best memories are of life in the South of the forties and fifties?

I am not sure I can answer these questions completely, and I am not sure I want to. Indeed, I can think of no more effective way to stifle inspiration than to theorize about the emotional sources of my plays. Still, one can hazard a few guesses. Because of my particular life history, my childhood memories just happen to be memories of the South before the civil-rights era. Since childhood memories have a special importance in everyone's life, perhaps no other explanation is needed. But I think something more is involved. Because racism was then legally entrenched and publicly justified, it was a significant accomplishment to build a life with cere-monies and rituals affirming the integrity and importance of our own friendships and families, of our own lives. In my childhood memories of life in the South, the world of the personal and the private, of everyday life with its ups and downs, is particularly important. To me this is a tribute to the tacit but adamant refusal of the grown-ups I knew to al-low themselves to be defined by racism but instead to live as full human beings, whatever the obstacles.

The cover photo was taken at the annual formal even-ing affair of my mother's bridge club, The Bridgettes, in my hometown in Tennessee in 1942 during the era of segregation. Many of the men in this photo were about to go off to serve in World War II. These men and women were all childhood friends and later school teachers, physicians, and funeral directors, people that gave so much to the African American community in our small town. Their formal dance was held in my uncle's workshop in back of his house, the same shop he used daily to repair and build furniture.

What has always struck me about this photo is the dignified, elegant, composed quality that shines through. These people seem radiant, engaging, and unstoppable. The figures in the photograph possess a quiet determination to find a place in their society, no matter what obstacles stood in their way. The men and women in this photograph refused to let their circumstances stop them from living their lives fully. My mother told me over and over again how important it was for her and her friends to dress well and, if need be, create their own occasions to put on all their best things, no matter what.

The notion of using a bridge game as a dramatic motif has been with me for a long time. I first tried writing plays in a course taught by Webster Smalley at the University of Illinois in the early sixties. Recently, while going through boxes of old manuscripts, I happened to find a copy of a scene that I had written back then; sure enough, it was one about a family playing bridge. Whenever I ask my creative writing students to recall a fragrance connected with some early memory, I give the example of the smell of spiced tea flavored with oranges and cloves, the drink served at the weekly meetings of my mother's bridge club. I was never allowed to stay very long at the club meetings, just long enough to smell the aroma of food and drink mixed with the odor of women's colognes, to feel a bit of crepe against my face and hear the quiet laughter. I remember the frustration of being forced to leave for a nap or whatever it was that good children were supposed to do. Perhaps my childhood frustration at always being on the edge of that world has motivated me to recreate the atmosphere for myself. Then I wasn't allowed to eat the shrimp salad sandwiches, rich with homemade mayonnaise, but now at least I can write about them in my play.

Although the content of *The Bridge Party* is derived from childhood memories of the American South, my dramatic treatment of those memories was influenced by films from France and Czechoslovakia. As a student at the University of Illinois in the sixties, I became interested in the foreign films that were shown by the campus film society. I was especially drawn to their use of understatement, which contrasted so sharply with the heavy-handed approach typical of Hollywood then and now. One film in particular, *The Shop on Main Street*, affected me deeply. A Czech film about the Nazi occupation of Czechoslovakia, it conveyed the impact of Nazism not by examples of brutality but instead through close attention to seemingly trivial details of everyday life. The film powerfully dramatized the impact of the Nazi occupation on the Czechs without resort to images of nattily dressed Gestapo officers or melodramatic violence, simply by depicting the everyday life of a shopkeeper and his wife. I was struck with the contrast between *The Shop on Main Street* and American films and television that so often glamorize the very evils they purport to condemn. The New Wave cinema of the fifties and sixties also affected me deeply. I remember sitting through Alain Resnais' *Last Year at Marienbad* over and over again, each time feeling more and more mesmerized. Resnais' powerful short film on the concentration camps, *Night and Fog*, exemplified the use of poetic understatement and pacing in presenting the most horrifying subject matter. The pacing characteristic of New Wave films, in which events were presented in a kind of slow motion, was a revelation for me. Through this slow motion, one confronted the particulars of individual experience rather than the abstraction of generalities.

If the action of *The Bridge Party* moves at what might at times seems to be a snail's pace, it is because I want the audience to experience the characters as full human beings, not as abstractions or stereotypes. I believe slow pacing allows for a depth of impact more meaningful than the most impressive stunts or special effects can achieve. For me as a playwright, the presentation of African American life in this style felt like a kind of glorious, liberating breakthrough as against the vast majority of films, television and plays dealing with African American life that focus on violence and/or sensationalized sexuality. Even in enlightened "message" dramas about racial violence in the South, it is typically only the whites who have the luxury of private lives. Over and over again black people are seen only in relation to whites, as though the whole identity of individual African Americans can be reduced to their reactions to racism. White people are presented as complex human beings with unique personal identities, but all too often, sometimes with the best of intentions, black people are portrayed only in moments of crisis, as though they had no private lives, no past, no inner depth. In *The Bridge Party* I wanted to both acknowledge the reality of violence, of lynching, and yet make it clear that the African American experience did not begin and end with the acts of violence perpetrated by others against African Americans.